A STONE'S THROW:

Inside the Stonefemme and Stonebutch Life

By Victoria Anne Darling

for my lovely stone man-friend
(and for all you man-friends)

May you always celebrate your stone

as deeply as I do.

Go. And stay.

Be free.

Let me love,

And be loved, as

You be you.

Stone (stōn)

Noun
1. Rock
2. Gem or precious stone
3. The hard covering that encloses the seed in certain fruits, such as a cherry, plum, or peach
4. Unit of mass or weight
5. A masculine non-male who dislikes being feminized (esp. sexually), and who partners with females: *stonebutch, stonestud*
6. Also: untouchable butch (genitally, sometimes also emotionally)
7. Also: touch-me-not stud (genitally)
8. A female who enjoys being feminized (esp. sexually), and who partners with masculine non-males: *stonefemme*
9. A female who is sexually aroused by and attracted to masculine non-male partners who generally or always decline penetration or genital contact, a few of whom experience their clitoris as the 'cock beneath their cock': *stonefemme*
10. Also: sexually/romantically accessible only to an untouchable butch or a touch-me-not stud: *stonefemme (also: stone for stone only)*
11. *Stone* community (see 5., 6., and 7.): *"We are stone"*; *"It's a stone event"*
12. Arrival at *stone* self-acceptance: *"My journey to stone was profound."*
13. *Informal.* Sweetheart; dear. Used as a term of endearment: *"Hey, stone, can I share your apple?"*
14. *Informal.* Something so remarkably fine that it is nearly untouchable: *a stone of a car*; *"That car is stone!"*

Proper noun
   Slang. A stonefemme or stonebutch: *"Come here now, Stone."*

Adjective
1. Relating to or made of stone: *a stone gate*
2. Complete; utter: *a stone liar*; *a stone identity*; *a stone woman*

Adverb

Completely; utterly: *stone cold; standing stone still; stone butch*

Verb

Slang. To set strong personal boundaries: *stone your way through it*

FOREWORD

This book is a collection of writings I wrote between 1994 and early 2004. While some of the content may seem rudimentary or behind the times with regard to where gender and sexuality conversations have made ground in recent years, its content is still helpful to those exploring the specifics and interior of the world and lives of Stones. I have chosen to let the entire collection stand as it is, with no material editing, so that those in the early stages of their self-discovery might better relate.

I imagine a field of wildflowers overlooking meadows and mountains on every side. In the center of this space is a structure: a circle of very wide stone pillars with an intricately carved stone dome arching across the tops. Within this formation the outside world fades and a magical moment in time opens, offering a sense of stillness and peace that envelopes me.

Inside these walls, I am protected and safe; free, if only for a short while, from judgments and confusion and harm. In this space, I can rest knowing I am fully accepted, fully alive, fully myself. In the profoundest sense possible, I am embraced. A warm light washes over me and chases away doubts, clears cobwebs of confusion, and resets me to my true self once more.

It is my wish that these pages become that shelter for you. Whoever and wherever you are, at whatever stage of stone identity, I hope these pages give you a sense of acceptance and safety. Linger here when you need comfort, when you want to surround yourself with others who understand, or when you want to explore the further edges of stone sexuality...at least my version of it.

Welcome home, stone wanderer.

Welcome home.

This book represents only one view and experience of being stone, although there are other equally valid versions. I've defaulted to "butch," rather than "stud," but only because it's the language I'm most comfortable using.

Please take what you like and leave the rest.

May you be loved (and wanted) beyond your wildest imagination –

exactly as you are right this moment.

Table of Contents

A STONE'S THROW:

Inside the Stonefemme and Stonebutch Life

Letter to Stones

How do I begin to tell you, what it means to me to be stone and love stone? There are so many nuances to convey, so much hope to share.

I heard it once said that "a femme is the only comfort this world offers a butch," and I believe that is particularly true for stones.

Power

It is a common misperception, that being feminine to a masculine counterpart means giving up control, standing in the background, or adopting a stance of deference and submission to our masculine partners. While some of us may embrace postures and opportunities like these, many of us do not. Some of us may feel comfortable adopting an auxiliary stance in public while retaining more aggressive or dominant characteristics in private or may vacillate between the two at will (or live fully at some set point between them).

What remains static for us all is *choice*. We each get the freedom to choose. We choose how we relate, how we position ourselves in community, and how we project ourselves in the world at large. That is where our real agency lies.

In a large number of stonefemme/stonebutch relationships, the partners enjoy a consensual exchange of power (aka Dominance/submission, also referred to as "D/s") – *in addition to* the power dynamics that accompany the butch/femme dance. Being a submissive femme does not automatically mean giving away the right to stomp your foot when you're mad, wanting your butch guy to take out the trash, or reining him in a bit when he needs it.

Likewise, being a dominant femme does not mean you don't bottom sexually, that you dislike being courted in old-fashioned ways, or that you want to direct your guy to shield you from the harshness of the world around you.

The power of being femme is not the same power of being

17

dominant (or submissive for that matter). They may go hand in hand for you, but they also might not.

Competency is an additional method of expressing power.

Most butch guys enjoy when the femmes in their life display and explore their competency, even when it occurs outside of traditionally feminine activities. The world is full of opportunities for men and masculine energies to display their prowess with competency – assuming leadership roles, using dangerous power tools, being "handy" around the house, etc.

Most women are socialized to bolster masculine egos (sometimes doing so in order to cover our own self-doubts and insecurities), which, unfortunately, often means deferring more complex or dangerous tasks to our partners.

The trickiest areas of relating are often those where the femme wants to exercise her competency or the butch wants to relinquish his. A femme may try to take over hanging the drapes or chopping wood so she can experience herself as someone with limitless power. Or a butch might like to see the power of his femme in action by not stepping up to protect her in small altercations.

When a femme takes over traditionally masculine duties unexpectedly it often has the effect of emasculating her butch partner. And a butch who foregoes traditionally masculine duties without warning will usually find he has (unwittingly) de-feminized his girl.

The idea here is to find ways to explore these areas so that neither partner thrusts the other person into foreign territory without power. Femmes and butches who take a little time to explain their intentions will get farther in achieving the outcomes they desire.

I was once double dating with another butch/femme couple. We were in my backyard on a wonderful balmy day sipping lemonade when the subject of a stump in my yard opened up. This stump was an ongoing source of frustration for me. The tree was cut long before I became a tenant, which was annoying enough due to its centralization within the yard, but much to my dismay it also sprouted unsightly spindly branches in every possible direction each spring. This two-foot adversary, just a foot in diameter, would grow dozens and dozens of long skinny arms often more than fifteen feet in length, awkwardly blocking the entire view of the yard.

So, we were sitting there, and I was once more lamenting my recurring landscape misfortune when the guys laughingly said they would pay good money to see me chop the limbs off. When I jokingly said I would if I had a saw, a sawzall was quickly produced along with encouraging instructions on its use. In no time at all my femme pal and I were thrilled to be buzzing off limbs wearing our sun dresses and wedge heels, much to the delight and cheers of our lemonade-drinking, shade-sitting butch dates.

We enjoyed exploring our competency in ways that *increased* our femininity – and it did not require "role-playing" to do it.

Femininity & Masculinity

Being feminine is not role-playing for femmes. The more feminized I become the more powerful I feel. I become a purer form of myself. It's like tuning the dial to get the clearest possible signal on the radio. The feeling is accentuated when my partners flex their masculinity and treat me in ways that that draw out and celebrate my feminine side. While I might feel more feminine when my partner enters a restaurant before me and leads me in behind him, you might like it more when the door is opened for you and you're invited to enter first.

The same is true for our partners; they need the same thing, only in reverse. Butch guys typically want us to let them protect us, climb ladders, and hang holiday lights. For many of them it accentuates their masculinity and sense of self and allows them to expand more fully into a way of being that increases their personal power and strengthens the masculine self-image that was denied them as a child and is the target of hate as an adult.

Let me reiterate this again: this is not about role-playing. It is about seeking and encouraging the activities that empower ourselves *and* our partners.

This applies during physical intimacies as well. I consider it my sacred duty to reference a butch's body and body parts (including their masculine attachments) in masculine ways. It's my privilege to open myself to him so he has on-going and consistent access to drink from me in the ways he needs to replenish, and I want to walk through the world seeking ways to guard his back and affirm his power wherever I can.

In some ways similar, I want the same from him.

I want him to treat my body with worship and reverence, cherishing the gift of my body's openness, and respecting my physical surrender or use of it during our intimacies. I may or may not do so in a submissive manner – but within stone sex, I am the recipient of his penetration and energy even if I am doing so from a position of taking rather than giving.

I aspire to be the best (stone) femme I can be. For me this means seeking ways to encourage my partner's masculinity, as I also seek to affirm actions that accentuate my femininity whenever and wherever I see them.

A Personal Exploration

I sometimes struggle with using my stonefemme identity in public forums because it seems to invalidate some of those I have loved and sexed with over the years. I feel protective of the intimacies we have shared, many of which involved great passion but little that was "stone."

I have been out an awfully long time and have had sex with almost all varieties of dykes (only once since then becoming intimate with a man, who was an FTM). The majority of those years I identified as a femme domme and (primarily) a sexual recipient. I was happy sexualizing butch boys and occasional femme girl bodies because of the power it gave me to touch their desire and massage them (no pun intended) toward my/our power-exchange goals. They had to open to me, and in that place, I was able to garner deep levels of surrender and high levels of erotic control. That does not mean I felt desire directly for their biological "parts" if you will. I felt desire for them, as a person, as an entity separate from me, as a gender, and as a source of power.

As I have aged, I have less interest in the discovery of non-stone surrender to me, and more in my own surrender to myself. I want to dig out the deepest parts of myself, see what it feels like to live with them on the outside, and revel in the wonderment of my desires, not revel in the wonderment of desiring, if that small distinction makes any sense to anyone.

The road narrows. With time, my understanding of myself gets clearer. I believe that I have always been a stonefemme, but I had to sift through a lot – and I mean a lot – of other identity aspects of myself to do so. Not to mention my partners' views and judgments of my identity, my religious and gender socializations, my relationship to power, and what defines sex and sexuality for me. There was also never any language for who I was and what I was attracted to.

I think fluidity can be like so many things; it must be taken in moderation. For my part, I was so proud of my ability to be fluid that I lost sight of my core sexual character and it has been a long road to recover it. I learned lessons and had great experiences – developed wonderful memories – but at what price?

I first used the term stonefemme for myself privately in 1998, and with others – very shyly – in 2002. In the two years since, I have discovered just how deep that river runs in me. It is no longer enough to say love comes first and what we do together sexually will be determined co-creatively thereafter.

I'm wired to fall in spinning-intoxicating-easy-to-fit-in-my-life-and-shared-vision-love with someone that I get to masculinize as much like a straight man physically and sexually as I can, all the while getting my rocks off on the fact that he's not: he's 100% queer.

I want the mirror experience in return.

I want to be sexualized as much like what mainstream society thinks is a straight woman and have him get off on my queerness underneath and within it. Without the queerness it is heterosexual sex (which is wonderful for those who are straight), but all the heat is robbed for me. It is the "kink" of having both that is the absolute hottest.

It is no wonder I fought against and searched for any other truth about my identity when "straight sex" was the closest language I had to define what I really want. I had to be seen as queer, too.

I liken being stone to tectonic plates; the endless rubbing of male/not male (and feminine female/not heterosexual female) energy creates an inner friction that is palpable and exhilarative and rich. If a stonebutch transitions to male all that beautiful, inner friction begins to resolve itself and they become something 'other', like heterosexual males are 'other' to me – and no stone heat remains.

On Self-Acceptance

Stone butches, and the women who love them, are incredible creatures. The identification of stone is usually empowering for those that choose or discover it. "Stone" does not come from a place of confusion or dysfunction, but rather from a fuller sense of self-awareness. Those that have embraced it incur a sort of magic, a strong sense of empowered "I know who I am and what I want," which can become added intensity for the femme who is drawn to strong counterparts.

I do not see why others, including mainstream lesbians, have referred to it as negative or aberrational. When a stone's identification comes from a place of healthy awareness and self-determination it is honey to flies, both femme and butch. Self-acceptance makes anyone stronger, particularly those who are stone.

I've found it quite pleasurable (and I hear the same from other sister-femmes) to be the one to assist my partners in accepting who they are, to assure them that it is okay to "be them". When one person stands as sentry and in full loving support of another's self-realizations, there is an intense and beautiful bond that occurs, the gift that the femme gives her butch, that reflects itself in the butch's eyes, his poise, his walk - that no one can ever take away from them again. It's that sense that they are not alone, and further, that there is (and always will be) a matched counterpart or partner for them - if they just look for it.

It is within that contrast (of stonebutch and stonefemme) that femmes often get to experience more intensity within their own femmeness. Kind of like the powerful frame that strikingly sets off the colorful canvas. Opposites are often the most similar. When stonebutches reach that level of identity ownership they become more autonomous, often standing stronger than they have their entire life, able to take on challenges that used to impede them. It is incredible to watch someone blossom.

Many times, femmes are mated with butches just to have

this blossoming occur between them and the relationship is then exhausted when the transformation is complete. In every case I have ever seen or heard of, when a stonebutch becomes fully realized, they are once again returned to that place called "at full choice."

It is a place where their unexposed identity begins to lose its place as the unresolved mental focus or nagging sense that something is "wrong with them". When they get to fully embrace themselves as they are then they can go on to use the energy their resolution has left them with to expend somewhere else. They then tend to go on and have a cleaner ability to decide how they want their identification to manifest itself. *They have more power to choose because they are not wasting energy wondering if they are flawed*.

They have full agency again...or maybe for the first time ever.

Freedom from unhealthy shame then occurs, and when it does that self-confidence that replaces it is sexy as hell.

I just keep going back to those times I've held a butch and said it's okay to be stone, saying it over and over until they get it – knowing, in their moment of self-realization when they look over to me and our eyes lock, that we are both okay and that the future is ours, both individually and collectively.

That is magic. Plain and simple.

Real Power Awaits

Dude, come with me
It's time
For you to join us
Enter our ranks
Learn to accept
What others
Most others
Disdain
And fight against

But today you will meet
The Girls
Those rare women
Who need us
Desire only
Us
You will meet
Your Self
In a new way

Your shoulders will square
Your stance will strut
Your manners
Will become
Sloppy or sharp
Depending

On the
Fellow
You are to be

Let me suggest the sharper path
Of the gentleman
Rather than
Rogue
The top-hat dandy
Rather than the leather jacket
Bum
That the ladies love

Maybe, just maybe
You will be
Both
Sometimes
Opening doors
Sometimes
Pinning them against one

Funny thing
They like both
Best

Your hardness
Opens their soft
Your manner

Blooms their beauty
Your gruff, their pride
And giggles
Let there be
More love
More beauty
More giggles

Come on, Dude
Become the one
She needs
Become the one
You were meant to be
There is no better
Now
There is no better
You

Only your
Real power

Awaits

Butch Vulnerability

James was still, after many years, trying to sort through his gender identity in an overwhelming sea of transsexual options and feelings of incongruence with his bio-female body. During one of our rare but lengthy coffee dates, we were walking along a pier when he mentioned that he had been struggling with a girl he was seeing about her being fine with his cock-identity in bed, but outside the bedroom she wanted him to be her "girlfriend" and refrain from packing. Though he might never have admitted it, I got the distinct feeling that he was indirectly looking for validation of his identity, in and out of the bedroom.

I stopped in my tracks, turned to him, looked him directly in the eye, and said very sternly, "Your cock exists whether you strap it on or not. It is always there and it always will be.

It is an organic part of you – a *permanent* part. Any femme worth her weight would see it and know it instinctively. No matter what you have or do not have in your bedside table drawer or your pants, it *always* exists. Always, always, *always*."

Though he doesn't cry, I could feel him choking up so I turned my face away to provide him privacy as I continued pattering about how any girl who wanted him to be something he wasn't comfortable with was espousing her own issues with gender. He could respect her best by not adjusting his identity to fit her perception of what it should be.

Another time, this same guy was at a party I hosted and he stayed late, with a few others, to finish playing a game that centered on asking people questions, sometimes very intimate ones. One of the other butches posed a question to the femmes as a group, "How do you deal with 'that time of the month' for butches?"

After the group threw out a few tongue-in-cheek remarks about 'getting out of their way' or 'handing them a pound of chocolate', I realized the butches in the room really needed to know. It was a sense more than a certainty, so I knew that however hard it might be for me, I had to step up. It was one of the more difficult social experiences I have been through.

My face turned a dark, dark red, my vision tunneled uncontrollably, and I became grateful for the dimmed after-party candlelight. I turned my focus to a femme I trusted and with a throat that kept threatening to seize up, I told her my experience because I couldn't tell it to them, the butches, though I knew they were listening.

I explained to her about how the straps from their harness, their 'other' cock (clit) when an attachment was not physically on their body, and especially their menses were invisible to me to the degree it made my partner most comfortable. I added that I would never, *ever* buy them monthly products unless I was asked directly or sensed that the experience was painful for them. But, if asked, it would only need to be once. From there forward the products would never be depleted, so they would never have to raise the subject again.

It was a matter of sacred discretion; I couldn't even tell this to them directly (the butches who'd asked) so I told this femme because I wanted to be sure they knew at least one person existed who wasn't intent on feminizing them or their body. The butches in the room watched in silence as I struggled to tell my much younger femme friend about how old-school femmes navigated the tricky waters and delicate souls of private gender politics.

I felt the guys get quiet and go still. I felt little parts of them heal. As silly as it sounds, I knew I was helping to make up a little for those who had not understood, and those who did not get it; those who did not get them.

I did not feel like I had a choice, as a femme who loved butches; it was my responsibility to tread with tenderness and love into places and topics that desperately needed to be understood and healed. Butches open to trust and femmes who care for them must live into the worthiness of that trust.

This kind of patience comes from someplace very deep in me. It sits behind the place where I take things personal, behind my own wounds and frustrations, behind judgments, behind filters and perceptions, and sometimes even behind desires for what I want.

I have to let go or suspend my attachment to all of these to really be there for the other person. I have to train myself to listen longer and deeper than my reactions. I've had to practice over and over and over sitting down, sitting on my hands, biting my tongue, not turning away emotionally, not moving sideways or backwards physically, and not avoiding the painful places their experience or words touch in me.

It is so extremely hard to do at times and even now, after loving so many butches as friends and partners, I still feel like I am still learning. I wish I could say I have not said or did things I regret, and that I somehow managed not to hurt those who trusted me, but that is not true. I am still fine-tuning my dance and, unfortunately, have stepped on a few toes and hearts in the process.

Damages

Whenever we talk about butch vulnerability (and the crustiness of the outer shells some of their hearts have) it's important to remember that even if it comes from a place of layered injuries it isn't okay is to patiently sit through rudeness or assault if it rises in them. What I mean by those two words is something very specific; Anyone who is aspersing you, ridiculing you in any way, spewing derogatory names, or intimidating you physically (including refusing to let you out of the room by blocking the doorway or refusing your right to a time-out) has deeper problems that need to be worked out with a therapist.

The way I see it is that when a partner lacks self-control and dumps or directs their pain and frustration at me, it is rude. It is deeply unkind to say around me that femmes are self-centered, that they are dumb or manipulative, or that I don't care about them (my partner) or don't try to get them. These are invalidating statements and it is never okay for my friends, and especially my intimate partners, to invalidate me as a femme, a woman, a person, or as a partner. There's a big difference in saying 'I'm struggling with these things' than stating them as fact.

The same goes for femmes toward butches. Butches are not inherently dense, stupid, thoughtless, controlling, or failures as humans so I don't have a right to relate to them that way. And I am personally responsible for shutting down any conversations with femmes or anyone else who wants to talk about them that way.

I am not perfect, but I do not get permission to be lazy with my language, to lash out, demean, or tease the love and patience coming my way, even if I want to. It's not so much that butches or femmes are so perfect or need to be held to such a high standard, but we do have to strive for it every day and clean up any messes we make along the path.

Perfection's impossible, but humility is not.

Softening a Femme

Imagine a woman, one you are (or would like to be) romantically involved with. See her smiling and happy every time you come near. Notice how she goes out of her way to entertain you, seduce you, and nurture you.

Maybe she tucks love notes in your boxed lunch. Maybe she seduces you into romantic picnics or surprises you with a lap dance late one evening when the two of you are alone. When you are stressed, she opens her blouse and lets you rest in her softness. When you place your head in her lap, she instantly begins to pet you. Or maybe she starts a giggling pillow fight on Saturday morning when you are eating cereal and watching cartoons.

She is playful, engaging, full of life and laughter, and fully confident in her sexual powers when she turns them on. And, she does all of these spontaneously, routinely, whenever the mood strikes her.

Or maybe she is not your romantic partner, but your friend. You can call her any hour day or night and she is always there for you, always supportive and encouraging and affirming.

When you say you are okay, she knows better, and gently calms and soothes you with her words or presence. She always knows exactly what to say at exactly the right time, giving you greater confidence and a stronger sense of purpose and your place in the world.

She also knows how to change the subject or distract you when a little reprieve is needed. You know without a shadow of a doubt that she always feels safe with you. She leans on you, trusts you, and knows you are in her corner no matter what comes. She makes you laugh. You feel stronger and more yourself in her presence.

These are all descriptions of a softened femme. She is warm and soft and open to you. With you she is confident and relaxed, even though the outside world sometimes trips her step.

Chances are if a femme has been like this and she is not anymore then it is possible you may have played a part in her emotional retreat.

But, the good news is, with time and persistence you may be able to get her back.

If you pay attention, most femmes (friends and lovers) will usually tell you what is required to keep them soft. She'll give you 'keys' that unlock her and free her to open to you this way. When you use these keys appropriately and sincerely (and at the right times) she will stay open too.

There are some keys that are common to femmes in general, but signature keys are the highest prized if you are smart enough to know you are holding them and aren't too stingy or afraid to use these gems.

These "keys" – the details that magically, mystically cause her to open her heart – are priceless. They give you power to have and know the woman within, and they also give *her* power when you ignite them. She becomes more of herself. She becomes *unleashed*.

Many falsely think that by learning a woman's likes and dislikes they will understand what really makes her tick. Those things are certainly useful, but they aren't remotely close to the power of her keys.

Let us consider the fairytale damsel, Rapunzel.

Rapunzel was towered away by an evil woman and needed someone outside to assist her escape. This tower had no out save for the locked stairwell. The only way anyone would be able to reach her was to climb up the outside of the tower. Rapunzel did not have a rope or thirty sheets she could tie together, so she had to get creative. She decided to grow her hair; a long braid that eventually reached the ground far below.

What kind of person would voluntarily put their entire weight on a woman's hair braid though? It is just not reasonable. They might break her neck. They might fall and kill them both. No way, *uh-uh*. Not going to happen, most people would be thinking.

But the realm's prince loved her and she him. They *wanted* to be together, and she had been trapped and held hostage for so long. There were just no other options available. If he did not climb up her hair, they would never be together, and worse, she would never get out. Her 'key' was that she needed him to *trust* her strength; that she could reach freedom, but only if he had the humility and willingness to climb up her hair first.

Can you imagine how she felt? Intuitively, Rapunzel knew her strength; she knew her hair and neck would hold. She needed him to take that risk, to let her participate in her escape. Maybe she "liked" chocolate and late-night TV, maybe she "disliked" snakes – but those likes and dislikes are not going to truly make her soften. You do not trust people just because they give you what you want and keep things away that you do not like.

Rapunzel had been controlled her entire life – unable to exercise her strength even once. It is certainly no wonder she wanted an opportunity to exercise her contribution.

Then there's Cinderella.

Cinderella had a fairy godmother and helpful, happy mice and birds. She did not really need a prince to gain freedom, even though the story might lead you to believe so at first glance. What Cinderella wanted was someone who could see past her poverty and ragged clothes. She wanted a prince charming like so many other girls – someone who would decline all other women *first* and then pick *her* out of the crowd; searching high and low to find her if need be.

Can you guess what her key was? Yep, it was the shoe she left behind. There is not a woman on the planet that loses a shoe she is wearing and does not know it. If it breaks or falls off she may kick the other one off too, but she doesn't go limping into the night in a ball gown wearing only one high heel without knowing it – no matter how upset or embarrassed she is.

Femmes who love butches leave their keys behind all the time. Sometimes it is a physical item; they leave a toothbrush or pair of panties, not to claim your space but rather to convey some subtle meaning that they want you to very sweetly draw them out about.

Often though it is a word or phrase, or way of touching them that matters most.

One woman I knew told her guy that when her neck was touched a certain way her body had an immediate and visceral reaction. Nothing she could do would prevent it.

Another woman shared with her partner that when he told her what he was about to do to her *before* he did it, she could not help but melt instantly. Funny thing is, neither of these guys pursued trying these things with them. They found it fabulously sexy to be told yet did not take note or consider for a minute that the women were telling them *for a reason*.

Not all keys are sex related.

Like the Cinderella and Rapunzel examples above, some keys are relational. If a woman says that her favorite thing in the world is someone who is kind in the face of insult, then you should immediately start working on your ability to control your responses in the face of difficult conflict. Just imagine how deeply her heart would be touched if you were able to bite your tongue and be gracious and kind the next time someone cuts you off in traffic or offends you in public.

Each woman has keys specific and important to her, but there are some more generalized softening techniques that will work with most femmes, so learning specific keys are not always paramount, though they *are* helpful in going even deeper.

I have listed the more general examples here to help jump start your thinking.

Remember, that while these are common to most femmes, they do not all apply to each one.

- **Physical flaws.** A femme friend I knew had one breast that was naturally smaller than the other.

She was very insecure about it, but like most women she did not point that out to new romantic partners. One fellow (a lover of large breasts) sensed her feelings about the smaller breast and declared on the spot it was his favorite. Each time they were intimate he would lavish much more attention on the smaller of the two, but he made sure he did so with sincerity.

Before long, the femme was proud of *both* breasts, and the soft spot she held for this fellow was incredible.

She knew, of all the people on the planet, she had found someone worthy of her body's gift, and her feelings of being cherished *exactly as she was* allowed her to blossom in his presence.

For another pal of mine it was a mole on her cheek she came to love, and for another it was a long scar on her forearm. By lovingly attending to their more vulnerable physical places these butches wooed the softness out of their femmes.

Most lovers can sense the places on their partner's body they instinctively hide or shy away from exposing, and lovers will generally follow suit in an effort to make the person more comfortable. But the smart (and exquisitely loving) partner will pick the right moment to turn the tables and bring even more kind and loving attention back to the exact spot of insecurity.

Every femme knows her physical weaknesses. Question is, how will you treat them?

- **Emotional strength.** We femmes may adore your strength, but we also like to feel ours. When you are strong physically, mentally, emotionally, and spiritually, we feel safer and more protected. But if you do not occasionally trust our emotional strength and actually lean on it from time to time, we cannot expand into the fullness of our selves.

Let me give you a fictional example.

Your mother (a wonderful, but enormously proud woman who adores your femme partner) is going through something physically painful right now. To protect her hip joints her doctor told her she would need to use a walker for the remainder of her life. She is devastated and yet she will not talk to you about it, and she has no one close to confide in. You know she needs support and a feminine woman's kindness and nurturing to open up. One day, after another unsuccessful attempt to reach out to her, you pull your femme aside and ask for her help. You lay out the facts and then you say, "I need you. You have insights and wisdom about feminine women that I will never have."

Your femme may intuitively know you are right and feel flattered that you asked but expresses that she feels uncertain. You respond with, "This is something you know you can do. If you do not want to, that's one thing, but I have confidence you know how to find the right words, and I believe you know it too. You can immediately sense the exact sore spot she's dealing with, and it's your strength she needs to see mirrored back to her."

Your partner desperately wants to help, so she agrees, and then discovers you were right. Despite her initial doubts, with your unwavering, rock-solid confidence in her ability, she is able to help your mother begin accepting that this new "dancing partner" will not take away from her beauty or regal bearing. Your mother's pain begins to bleed away and your femme returns happy and proud to have completed the mission you sent her on, which translates into an even greater softness in your arms.

- **Loyalty.** Femmes thrive when those closest to them are devoutly loyal. Hearts are tender things but they soften easily when someone fiercely steps up to protect them.

It is not just an internal loyalty that moves them; it is when that loyalty is publicly or outwardly expressed.

Refusing to share her private routines and habits when you're with a group who is discussing their own, being trustworthy with her secrets, defending her honor simply because you've chosen to stand with her even without knowing every detail of the conflict – these are just a few ways this kind of fierce loyalty is displayed.

These expressions of loyalty will always begin to melt any crust formed over her heart.

- **Pride.** This is an especially important component, and a powerful method of softening a woman. When I say pride, I am not referring to the pride you might have in yourself or the pride of stance or carriage, but rather sincere pride of her and all of her achievements.

  I have never met a femme who did not melt the minute she heard her favorite guy sincerely express tremendous pride in what she has overcome, or accomplished, or in how she looks to others. We all need that kind of affirmation from our lover.

  One gal I knew struggled with a few extra pounds was teased about her high calorie dessert by a friend, and her guy instantly popped up and said (with a warm wink in his eye and a happy grin stretching across his face) that she didn't have to watch her weight because *he* did that for her. He managed to sound like her body, in whatever state it was right now, could not be more perfect exactly the way it was.

- **Feminization.** Ball gowns, perfume, flowers, shoes, hair combs, and trinkets. Or, maybe flavored Chapstick, girly ball caps, wildflowers, and ponytail ties. What makes a woman feel feminine varies from one gal to the next, but the focus is the same when you are talking about keys.

As long as women know you see and value their inner strength and competency, they generally swoon at being treated like a feminine girl, a princess, a queen, or a grande dame. Gifts like these do not always open a femme or initiate her softening, but when delivered authentically without ulterior expectation they will usually expand any seeds of softness that have already been planted.

You may think you already do these things, but if you are not doing them the *way* that matters to that particular femme, she will not be able to recognize and benefit from them. You might *feel* you are loyal or proud of her, but if she doesn't see it then it won't ignite the openness you're seeking.

If you're not paying attention, a woman's heart will distance itself from you each time she has to protect it from your harsh words, abrupt emotional withdrawal, or failure to extend understanding and compassion to see her side of things. She will also lose faith and softness when her keys are ignored or go without being seen. This distance is not a means to punish you; it is simply her method of ensuring her ability to open later is safeguarded. She has to withdraw at least somewhat or the fullness of her giving will become damaged.

No femme can give into a vacuum for an extended period of time. And they certainly cannot remain soft and open with someone who is neglectful, dunce-minded, cruel, or lacking in self-control.

None of us are perfect. No one will always see all the keys that are laid at their feet, nor will they always remember to use them – we usually have too much 'stuff' to set aside our own ego and take the risks required. All too often we rely on methods of relating that we think work for us, when in actuality they may be the very things that close down those we hold most dear.

If I were a guy and I wanted my girl to stay soft for me –

to open to me whenever and wherever I needed to the greatest capacity she had to open to anyone – then I would start a list. Do perfume and flowers after an argument make her giggly and soft? Do sweet notes on her pillow each morning make her cry? Or is it being kind to strangers in need that deepens her admiration of you?

What would it really cost to offer a few bucks to a homeless man when you are with her, even if it went against your usual comfort zone or personal mores? Purchasing a new scent for Valentine's Day is nice, but if it matters so more that she receives it as an apology after her feelings have been hurt, shouldn't a new bottle (or perfume samples from a magazine) be tucked away now before it's needed?

The softness of a woman's heart is a place where butches go to rest. Inside that softness they are sheltered and protected; nourished and replenished after all storms.

Unfortunately, some guys see giving femmes exactly what they want as a weakness.

Try not to be one of them.

Don't Tone It Down

Countless times over the years
You have chosen to wear
Something less
Hard
Something less
Specific
Something less
Male

You have been told by
Trusted lovers
Frightened mothers
Concerned fathers
And even your closest friends
To dress
Less obvious
Less overt
Less masculine

Even without thinking
You've
Searched your closet
Questioning
Will this be
Too much
Too noticeable
Too butch

Are you crazy?

Did you know I scan

Grocery isles

Theaters

Parking lots

Government lines

For someone like you

Each day is a new conflict waiting to face.

How many will mistake my feminine for weakness

How many will reach out to touch what isn't theirs

How many will count me with the moral majority just
because of how I look

Seeing you in a crowd of strangers makes all the difference
in the world.

Finally

Heart racing

Blush creeping

Breathing deepened

I am

Alive

Sexier

More powerful

Less

Invisible

Less

Straight-seeming

Less

Wasted

Being able to see you means

I am not alone

It is my proof

That I am not one of them

Not

Made for a man

But rather

Made

For a butch

Please don't tone it down

Maybe we will never meet and

I will not get you into my warm bed

Maybe we will never be friends

Co-conspirators

Or confidants

But even so

You will still be

My champion

Hero

Brave knight
My renegade pirate

In my dreams
And on the street
You make it worth
Being femme

So, square your shoulders
Pull out your bad-boy-rough-trade self
Be that Dapper Dan you have kept hidden
Don your "obviously male"
And let the butchest part of you move up to
Start riding in the front seat.
Don't tone it down – So that I
And others like me
Can
Find you
Love you
Sex you
Drink from you
Whether you know
We are watching
Or not
No matter what you do
Don't, don't, *don't*
Tone it down.

Mechanical Sass

When I was 20 or so, I took my car in for servicing and was promptly met with an unscrupulous invoice, one that depleted my meager life savings at the time. Within a few weeks, I enrolled in an automobile mechanics' course that stretched eight hours a day, five days a week, for six thrilling months.

In that brief time, I turned rotors, gapped spark plugs, and successfully diagnosed Freon systems (long before R134 was the industry standard). I even removed and replaced the engines of a classic Mustang and an Opal, the latter of which stumped my team dead until the teacher saved us by revealing we would have to hoist the body *over* the dropped engine rather than extract it upwards in the traditional manner.

I missed not one moment of class, though I did quit during the last week once the learning had ceased and the emphasis to gain employment took its place. While I had momentary visions of opening and owning a 1950's style station, with a crew of women technicians in vintage baby-girl pink coveralls with unquestionable ethics that defied the industry stereotype, it passed rather quickly once I realized what the work was doing to my nails.

I have never been screwed on a mechanic's bill since.

Most mechanics now do not know quite what to do with me. Which is how I like it.

I once wrote a ditty of a story about a femme who put each suitor in turn through a test on their first date to determine her interest in any future with them.

Requesting them each to drive her car, she had surreptitiously loosened a radiator hose clamp, just enough, but not too. When the car overheated, as it was wont to do with lessened water, she immediately offered to take a peek, noting a little experience and a brother's tools in the trunk.

She found one date unreasonably enraged at the audacity

of the car's breakdown, another who demanded *his* femme not exit the car (though he could do nothing), one who left her helplessly stranded whilst he went for help, and still another who called immediately for a tow. Without exception, each unforgivably refused her offer of aid and each was absolutely convinced the ailment was terminal (due more to assumption than knowledge).

It was the sole fellow thrilled at her abilities and a two-minute tightening of the clamp that won her heart.

Silent Voices

We had seen each other once before, at some poolside party long ago. You had worn a tuxedo jacket and shirt with jeans and boots, I'd worn a sequined dress; we were the only two overdressed for the event, obviously arriving late from destinations unknown. Our eyes met briefly several times in the short period we were both there, in acknowledgement and question.

We each seemed intent on avoiding an introduction; slipping away whenever we seemed too close to a conversation shared. You were well known and liked among the guests and appeared to submit your vanity to others' wherever they sought attention for subject or self.

I liked your manner, and went home quite curious, wondering if you were about me as well.

Now, here you are at the theater, alone, as I am.

As the intermission lights go up and patrons begin to mill, I notice you in the box directly across from mine. You notice me a moment later. We nod. The gentleman on my right just beyond an empty chair says something, and I am momentarily distracted. When my gaze returns you are gone.

I stand, straighten the navy sheath I have worn, and turn to exit the isle. I smile and nod to those I vaguely know and walk the length of the corridor toward one of the more central beverage stations. I want to ensure I have a view.

Red wine secured; I make my way to the lobby balcony overlooking the crowds below. I casually scan the mingling groups, feigning disinterest, and boredom, yet I feel an excitement the evening's entertainment has not provided me. My lips barely touch the wine when I feel your presence appear quietly next to mine. It is all I can do not to portray how startled I am, nor how pleased.

Never turning to acknowledge you, I keep my eyes on the crowd. I try to steady my pulse, and take another slow, careful sip of my wine. I let our bodies adjust to this new proximity. To your credit you do not speak. After a few moments, I turn and walk away.

I return to my seat late, just after final bells have been rung, sensing you are already in yours. In the last moment before the lights go down, I let my program fall seemingly by accident to the floor in front of me, near the railing. Before the gentleman nearest me can react, I move forward in my seat and lean down to get it, revealing cream curves in the deep V of my dress as I do.

Just as my hand reaches the program, I pause. I bring my head up and look directly at you, holding still for the barest second. In that poised moment I flash a brilliant smile, one intended to disarm, knowing full well the view you have been given. As the lights dim and the curtains begin to ascend, I look away. And I sense my sweetened arrow has hit its mark, dead center.

The second intermission finds me again at the balcony's railing in the lobby, though this time I have positioned myself with my back to one of the pillars. I smile watching you approach. I let you walk fully up to me and then stand there facing me as we speak our silent hello. I note your eyes, your dimples, and your lips, before returning to your gaze.

You watch me watching you, and then follow my eyes as I glance to the elevator and back to yours. Your smile is my response.

I walk away, and this time you follow.

Upon entering the lift, I push the button for Lower Level 4. As others exit the floor before ours, I let them assume I am departing the festivities early as they bid me, and my silent escort, goodnight. When we reach our destination, we are alone.

I step out of the car and turn right; heading straight for the emergency stairwell I know will be empty. Your footsteps echo behind mine.

Once inside I turn to you, reach for your lapels to pull you close, and move backward toward the wall. Your mouth reaches for mine and I turn my face. I will not give kisses to someone I do not yet know. Your hands reach to pull my hips roughly forward, and I moan softly against your shoulder. I can feel the rush of your blood through your clothes. I dip my head downward to your upper arm and open my mouth to bite through your jacket. I know I will not break skin, but I intend to crush it a bit in my need.

In blinding pain, you struggle to control your howl, and respond instantly by forcing your knee between my thighs, causing the skirt of my dress to slide up as you do.

Your mouth finds my neck, and my head lolls back in pleasure, releasing your now bruised and throbbing arm. I gasp as your tongue makes it affects known, my right fist now pounds against where once I had bitten, and my left hand reaches down to drive your knee deeper.

All at once your mouth opens wide, your teeth descend, and your jaw locks solidly around my throat. I freeze, my eyes flashing open in surprise, but not without noting your skill and marveling with certainty that there will be no remaining mark tomorrow.

But this is not tomorrow. And right now, I am held still at the mercy of your teeth against my jugular, much like a kitten to its mother. I can do nothing but let you ravage me; your knee slams upward against me, my thoughts a swirl within my alternating gasps and moans, and my hands grasp for anything steady to hold.

As my climax approaches, my right thumb digs deep into the tender flesh of the bite, and the shooting pain it causes you spurs you even more. Until finally, I peak. I can remember my name no longer.

Sated, I slump against you weakly, your teeth and the bite long forgotten. The presence of your knee retreats without notice. Almost, that is. I am still flushed and try to regain my sense of self with my face still against your shoulder.

Your hands are gentle as they smooth my skirt down.

With my palms upon your chest and your arms encircling my waist, I lean back to look you in the eye, chuckling in pleasure as I do. Your grin beams bright and we share our moment as two old friends, reunited after long, hungry months apart.

Then, as my hands reach up to check the status of my hair, you step back, watching. You bend down to retrieve the clutch I dropped early on, and I nod and smile my approval as I receive it. I open its crystal closure, reach inside, withdraw a small white card, and drop it on the floor as I turn and leave without looking at you again.

I feel you grin behind my departing back.

Owned

Our eyes met
I
Could
See

N
O
T
H
I
N
G

Else

You moved toward me
Slow
Deliberate
Steps

Held me
In your
Stone
Power

My knees
Weakened

My internal wrists
Turned
Up

Then you were there
Standing before me

Speaking
Without
Words

Seeing
Me

And I was

Yours.

Montana

Stand tall
my butch
hold my need
my shape
my gaze

Size me up
then
size
your ego down

Use the night air
cold
the stars,
the hue
to touch me past
my
barriers
my mask

Sing a melody of movement
across my
mind
my body
feel me

open
wet
and healed

Monikers and Semantics

Stone Identities

Several lovers have taken note of how easily I have embraced their masculinity and expressions of stone sexuality and then asked me, sometimes with an accusatory tone, if I was actually straight – always just after our throes of ecstasy.

The emotional pain this always caused was rather acute, not because it might be true, but because it divided us in the moments and areas where I was most devoted and supportive.

It is taken some time, but I have come to realize the question had more to do with their gender confusion and lack of self-acceptance than mine.

At every level, the question devalues me a stone femme.

It conveys there could be no one and nothing to love about that which my partners are – a masculine entity residing within a biologically assigned-female vessel. It communicates rather directly that if I were smarter I could have found a way to get a "real" man, that I'm hiding latent feelings of heterosexuality, that I have not been extensive enough in my self-examinations, and that my contributions to our stone interactions are invalid and false.

Maybe they did not mean it that way. Maybe they meant to say, "Honey, I'm scared. As stupid as it sounds, I am afraid if I continue to explore this part of myself, it will cause you to want more than I come equipped with. I still have fears that I will never be completely what you need and maybe one of these days you'll abandon me for someone who has more.

Can you stand with me while I face these demons and learn how to slash them down to a manageable size? I promise to do my best to protect you. I love you and you are important to me. I just don't want to lose you by pushing you away."

If the Goddess in all her eminence and compassion could create a stone butch, wouldn't she also create for him a counterpart? One that did not *want* a biologically assigned-male vessel, but rather the dichotomy – the heat, the "rub" and friction – that is caused when a masculine gender is trapped or housed inside a female-assigned body? Wouldn't that goddess also ensure our bodies responded to a stone butch's sexuality *specifically*? Couldn't we be designed in such a way as to actually *prefer* fingers, a fist, and especially a latex attachment much MORE than a biological penis?

Your attachments are biologically normal to us. You are wired to fulfill our every need. Your natural state in and with the body you were given is our perfect counterpart.

Anything else would be unnatural.

Most religions say that physical coupling of anyone other than a male-to-female union is immoral. I say it is immoral for me to be with a biological male. It is not natural to me chemically or physically, and I believe She created my wiring for a reason.

So that I might be the Eve to my stone butch's Adam.

Pronouns

I have a private preference for traditional masculine pronouns for and about my partners, especially when I am with friends and family who understand me. He, him, fellow, guy, stud, husband, boy, and occasionally dude feel most natural and affirming to me. The way I see it the stone guys in my life have spent so much of their waking lives unaffirmed for their masculinity, the least I can do is find ways to acknowledge it as completely as possible.

That doesn't mean I have to use these if they prefer female, they/them/their, or hy/hym/hir pronouns, or that I can't slip naturally into female pronouns when I am engaging with them around others who don't understand us. But I *like* encouraging their masculinity and affirming their queerness. Though this may not translate well, masculine and queer pronouns also help me feel and affirm my own queerness. I feel my queerness more accurately when I use them.

One other benefit of using these pronouns is that on a very subtle and private level it has the added bonus of reaffirming my difference from lesbians. Don't get me wrong, some of my favorite people in the world have been lesbians, and I have such a profound love and appreciation for women that I could easily play one on TV, but a lesbian I'm not.

Lesbianism, as I see it, is primarily about two "like" souls loving each other; two female-identified women in a romantic and sexual exchange. But my partners are not wholly female, and I'm not wired to prefer someone who is wholly female. In stone sexuality, I am not like my partner, and in many ways, we are polar opposites – not heterosexual gender opposites, but genderqueer opposites.

In my world, wanting a masculine entity inside and expressed through a female body could never be considered true lesbianism.

I do, however, like the word "dyke".

For me dyke encapsulates the intensity, the 'otherness', the sexuality, and the queerness of who I am. It's hard and rough and sexy. It seems to embrace the differences and turn them into raw power. It conveys that the dial has been zeroed into its most pure form and what is channeled through as a result is exciting, passion-filled, and *hot*.

I always adopt it for myself even when it does not entirely work for all my partners.

Bitch and Whore

When used privately and with the right inflection and intent, these are often two of the sexiest words that can be delivered to a stone femme. Not with all of us mind you, but certainly with quite a few. When used appropriately they are an excellent form of foreplay on the days we like it a little rougher.

Though the word "bitch" has long be used in derogatory

ways within the heterosexual community and refers to a woman who does not know her place, is extremely difficult to cooperate with, and/or adopts and uses power in ways that are uncomfortable to men – for us it is just the opposite.

Most femmes like to feel their personal power and see exercising it as a gift and a way of also affirming the power of our partners. The more sexy and powerful we are, the smarter, sexier, and more powerful our partners must be for choosing us. We enjoy taking up the fullness of the space we were granted on this planet, and though we don't need to infringe on your space (unless you like that sort of thing) we do see expressing our power as an act of self-fulfillment.

Likewise, the classic use of the word "whore" was used exclusively to verbally punish women who made sexual choices outside the accepted norm, whatever that happened to be at the time. It was the strongest way possible to communicate disproval and foster shame in women who often exercised the very same freedoms as men.

"Whore" meant you had strayed from the Madonna-like restraints all women should be happily chained within. It also meant you acted in ways so devaluing to yourself that you deserved to be ostracized in some way until you resolved the internal issues that led to your separation from a more wholesome and socially acceptable lifestyle.

While I do believe part of being femme is to nourish and protect the Madonna-like spirit within me, that is only one aspect of my sum. Some women need to explore the fullness of this Madonna part in all aspects of their life, and thus will likely not appreciate use of the term bitch or whore, but there are others of us who want to bring light into all areas of our darkness. We don't have a desire to be indiscriminately promiscuous, but we do want to give ourselves permission to be as intensely sexual (and sexualized) as we can be within the realm of our romantic partnerships.

If we were actually whores or bitches in the classic (and derogatory) senses of the words, we would not want to be called these things – especially within our most trusted private exchanges.

When a butch has a deep and abiding love and appreciation for females, it seeps out of his pores. We can tell. When that type of fellow asks us or consensually demands from us to be his whore for the evening – and we know he would be devastated if he harmed or devalued us in any way – then we're freed up to explore the edges of our sexuality and the fullness of our sexual power. We can go places we couldn't go otherwise. We can take risks because we know he would fight to protect us from any harm – especially from himself.

When you love and worship women so much that you could never use these terms in a disparaging fashion, we know it.

Just like we get that using "him" and "he" does not qualify you as heterosexual male or demean your queerness, so too words like "bitch" and "whore" (when delivered with sexy banter, appreciative power, and consensual sexual demands) do not disqualify or discount our purity.

Agreeing to be a lover's whore for an evening is a sacred pledge to give myself as fully and unreservedly as possible, while owning every ounce of my power as I do.

I just takes a very secure and confident guy to play with these edges and give us the freedom to go there.

Femme Invisibility

How many of these examples have you seen?

- ✓ Your femme understands your social discomfort with strangers and steps forward to make introductions and lead the conversation

- ✓ You come home angry and frustrated with the day and your girl offers you a haven and encouragement, but only when you are ready to welcome it

- ✓ You are shy on your first few dates with someone so the woman you're interested in devises question and answer games that leave you alternating between rolling in laughter and being erotically charged

- ✓ Your femme partner reveals one of her vulnerabilities simply so you will get to know her better

- ✓ Your femme asks you gently if you are okay, only to discover you're not. She then carefully draws you out so you can talk about it and release the stress

- ✓ Your girl whispers a code word only the two of you understand right before you do something stupid or embarrassing, helping you avoid public disaster

- ✓ "Monthly" products magically appear on the bathroom shelf before they are needed

- ✓ Your girlfriend discreetly looks away and seems not to notice when you fumble with getting into your harness, or she caresses your arms or upper back as she whispers low, sexy words to you that feel encouraging and make you feel stronger

There are a thousand different ways femmes step up to make your path more comfortable and easier. She adjusts so you do not have to. She draws you out when you cannot come forward emotionally or don't realize you need to. She makes a space in her life where you feel safe and strong and right. When you argue she bites her tongue, apologizes first, and often assumes the greatest degree of responsibility for the break down.

These are all examples of skills that are too often invisible.

But there are other ways she is invisible.

In addition to not having her gifts noticed within her intimate encounters, she is also missing from the visual pages of mainstream thought. Each day you enter a women's restroom and deal with the hassling looks of fear or disgust, but she enters the same room and no one notices. If she were heterosexual it would acceptable and right to assume she was as well, but she is not.

Each day that the oppressing world conveys to you that your differences are wrong, she is receiving an equally vehement message to stay hidden that is even more deadly in its silence. You are acknowledged for your queerness and given the opportunity to fight your oppressors head on, but she is quietly forced and encouraged to "pass" and slip through as something she's not.

You have the 'privilege' of being seen, she has the 'privilege' of going unnoticed; equal remainders of separate injustices to be sure.

Unless she decides to make a point of telling everyone she comes in contact with who and what she is, she is given no chance to claim her space as a queer woman outside of her home or community. Her only other option is to be *less* feminine, and to adopt more masculine attire, as Lady Troubridge did for Radclyffe Hall in Victorian times, so as to proclaim her sexuality more publicly.

The consistent message she receives is that her differences are not acceptable, and, because this message is delivered subliminally, it is all too easy for femmes to internalize without ever realizing it.

She is invisible to the world, and her gifts, her essence is invisible to you, her lover.

So, if she is not safe outside your arms and she is not seen or appreciated fully within them, then how does she refuel? What does she have left for herself when she has extended her softness and strength to you in ways you don't stop to acknowledge (and often act as if you feel entitled)? What does she have remaining when the outside worlds chips away at the pride of her identity?

In a low budget documentary, a butch filmmaker carries, sets up, and shoots the camera. He loads and unloads the car and he works at being technically proficient at operating the equipment. But the femme he hired to interview the subjects is called "the talent." She is the one who puts the subject at ease, the one who gets them to open up and take risks, the one who safeguards their heart and privacies. She is the one that makes the story come alive.

Without her, the story is dull and lifeless; a series of images blurred across the screen as the watcher falls asleep. The interviewer explores the tensions, senses when it is best to push deeper, asks the provocative questions in ways that do not offend, and strategically maneuvers the delicate intricacies of intimacy even with relative strangers.

You certainly enrich her life, but it is the femme's *invisible* dance that enriches yours.

What will you do to protect, respect, appreciate, and acknowledge her contributions? What will you do to soften her when she is tired, angry, or worn out from the world?

What will you give back to friends who are femmes? Will you be one of those guys who continue to receive these gifts without recompense, thinking them your due?

Femme Beauty Contest

The first time I visited a lesbian bar I was in for quite a shock. Without exception everyone there wore flannel shirts, jeans, had extremely short hair or wore a mullet. I had no way of knowing that first year that it was simply a blue-collar bar, and that there were other options available.

My first girlfriend took me a couple of times a week, mostly off-hours or weeknights. The more I visited, the more convinced I became that I would have to cut my hair (it was waist length at the time), buy a truck, and wear my keys on my belt loop to get a date if I were ever single again. I shuddered at the thought. Heck, I did not even own a pair of pants...how would I ever get noticed?

Some months later, after my girlfriend and I broke up, I decided to hell with staying at home and feeling sorry for myself, I was going out. And I did not care if I got thrown out for how I looked, I was going to wear what I felt most fabulous in.

I decided on a double-breasted, plunge-neck, black velvet skirt suit, stopping just above my knees, with wide satin lapels, and no blouse beneath. Black velvet stilettos, seamed stockings, and a bare hint of rhinestones at each ear and one wrist. My hair in soft curls around me, red lipstick and nails finishing it off.

When I walked in the bar everyone turned and stared. It was a Friday night, and I was the lone femme in a sea of butches (though I did not learn those terms until later). The power of that moment, when I walked in, brass balls to the wall, and made my way to the bar and ordered a drink, was incredible. I dared anyone to throw me out or make fun of my differences. I was terrified but damned if I'd let anyone see.

I had no idea that experience was incredible for others as well, but it was not long before I understood how much so.

Not knowing what to do with myself, I put two quarters up

on the pool table. I figured it would keep me from looking pitiful and lonely, giving me something to do.

I have never seen so many quarters laid down after mine so fast. They nearly went round the table. Very quickly, I began to feel like Scarlet O'Hara, and I had an evening unlike many others. Quite the femme's fantasy to be sure.

My femmeness, if it was not already, was set in concrete that night. Though many through the years have hassled me for it, I never once doubted it again. I am certain I could never be anything else.

Over the next few months, I had my choice of dates. Did I want to date someone tall? No problem. Someone funny or sexy? Someone with blue eyes? Whatever I wanted, I got. I did not sleep with many of them, but I sure was shown a good time. I seemed to be the sole oasis they had been starved for.

One night, on a date with one of these fellows, we walked in the bar and immediately the featured singer made a big to-do by dedicating a song to me. "You've got my number, you've got my name, why don't you call me, Liza Jane" he sung while pointing straight to me, much to my flustered chagrin.

In the midst of that song, and while trying not to show too much enjoyment of the flattery in deference to my escort, another butch took advantage of my date turning to get me a drink by jumping up on the pool table in front of me. He too joined into the live performance as he also tried to get my attention and lure me away.

I was surrounded, and it was hard not to laugh delightedly as I shooed them. I tried hard to focus on my date, which happened to be quite a bit less attractive than either of the competing crooners.

But I focused my energy and attention and did the right thing. What kind of gal would I be if I went off with either of them? Not one I would like, certainly.

So, this was the environment that encouraged me to run

for the Ms. Femme contest.

Don't laugh.

The bar had about as horrid a name for a dyke bar as you can imagine, but unfortunately it was the best of the two options available to me – the other dyke bar in town was named something even worse if that were possible. (Why do our bar owners do that anyway?)

The preparation for the contest was intense, but the event itself was a blast. Three categories, four gowns, and endless accessories, as my hair was styled by one of the best gay men in town.

Formal presentation found me in a black strapless ball gown ala *The King and I*.

Q&A session was in a sheer red lace Victorian with a remarkably high neck and pearl closures down the back and from elbows to wrists, with my hair in a French twist.

I honestly cannot recall what I wore for the award portion, but it was the talent segment that took the roof off the place.

I am not sure if you are familiar with Reba McEntire, but her song *Fancy* was a hit right about the same time as Melissa Ethridge's *Like the Way I Do*. Remember that one? Gosh I loved that song.

Anyway. *Fancy* is a story-telling song, one that has a sort of an *Unsinkable Molly Brown* theme. The story starts off with her in abject poverty, but she goes on to learn how to become and have everything she ever wanted. It is in the red velvet dress that she wears that becomes her ticket out, so of course I recreated the dress for the part, and wore it hidden under a tattered old lady's housecoat until the big reveal.

Now I don't know what the dyke bars are like in your neck of the woods, but where I lived the butch/femme performers are expected to lip-sync to songs unless they have incredible voices, which is rare, and which I don't have.

The song was culturally a great choice for the bar I was in. And the place was so packed that there was not even any standing room; people were trying to lean in from outside to see.

Everyone there loved the song, and I have never in my life heard such thundering after I was done.

Boots stomping on the floor, fists and yes, even folding chairs banging against walls, deafening cheers that did not seem to quit.

The competition looked at me backstage when I was done and knew immediately it was over. I was so high when I was done, so affected by the response; I was jumping up and down in heels and evening gown and screaming at the top of my lungs just to release the energy. But no one ever heard me over the crowd out front. There was just too much noise.

The bar owner came backstage looking discombobulated and seemed to not know quite how to handle the ruckus that would not die. He looked a bit like he was not sure if I should go out for an encore (which isn't done in contests) or if the crowd was going to tear his place apart if I didn't.

I won first place.

And although I would never want to do something like that again, I am so very glad I did it.

What a great affirmation of my femininity.

A Close Shave

I smiled as you walked in, a wide grin that hid secrets, promised excitement, and conveyed both pride and pleasure. I nodded as you took your seat, motioning for you to lean back and relax. You folded the copy of the *Times* you carried with you and placed it across your lap, then lay your head in the red leather cradle of my antique barber chair, closing your eyes almost instinctively as you did.

I could scarce believe you were finally here, after all the wanting, all the waiting and hoping. Never before had you agreed to sit in my new chair, submitting yourself to the skills I assured you I practiced endlessly to earn.

I shook the drape open, snapped it lightly for a little flourish, and then clasped it closed over the towel I had placed around your neck. I pressed a foot pedal to raise the chair a little higher, then a handle to recline. I opened the small warming cabinet, pulled out a wet towel, folded it in half lengthwise, and placed it carefully around the lower half of your face.

Then I pulled out a second towel and repeated my steps, placing this one gently around your forehead and over your closed eyes. The towels were scented lightly with lavender, and I left you to your quiet moment as I moved to complete my preparations.

As you settled in from the distractions of the day, I began pulling out the things I needed in the careful and ritualistic way I had learned. I laid a dry, fresh, scented hand towel across your chest; then another on the table beside us before pouring a pitcher of heated water into the silver bowl.

Beside the bowl I set out my leather strop, a tub of glycerin-based shaving cream, a beautiful English badger shaving brush, my porcelain bowl for shaving cream, and a pearl- handled antique straight razor in its velvet lined case that had purchased especially for you.

First, I opened the case and removed the razor, and then I turned to pick up the strop. I began by sliding the blade back and forth, until I was comforted by its careful slapping echoing gently in our room.

Once I was convinced it was sufficiently sharp, I wiped each side of the blade on the towel hanging at my waist and returned it closed to the table.

Quietly, I began mixing the cream and allowed the bristles to whip the lather up into fragrant foam.

Moving with care, I gently withdrew the towels from your face and began to apply the cream. In slow, circular motions I started by coating your right cheek, then sliding the brush sensuously down your jaw line, under your chin, and, with deliberate slowness, moved it in small circles across the strong neck I'd come to love so much.

Finally, I moved my brush to attend your left cheek. Feeling the intensity with which you were paying attention, though your eyes remained closed, I wondered for a moment what you were thinking.

As I leaned across you to finish the farthest reaches of my careful ministrations, the full softness of my chest pressed against your arm. You managed to remain completely still; the slight flare of your nostrils and tightening of your jaw the only indication you had noticed.

I enjoyed this moment and our closeness more than I expected; my face flushed and my breath softly quickened. It became significantly harder to concentrate. I have to focus, I told myself as I tried to recall what came next.

After setting aside the bowl and brush, I reached for my razor.

I pulled open the blade again, rested my index and middle fingers across its back, placed my ring and pinky fingers in the grooved tang that curved out just above the joint, and put my thumb slightly against the sloping shoulder just before the point where it became the blade. I paused momentarily, mentally running through the checklist of next steps.

Then I stepped forward again, blade poised.

On my free hand, my thumb rested against the crest of your cheek, ready to stretch it taut. Just before the blade came down, your left hand snapped out unexpectedly and encircled my wrist tightly. Your eyes flashed open at me, and I felt caught, suspended in mid motion, unable to breathe.

You let the moment linger and lengthen as your eyes held mine, the warning apparent and palpable. My face flushed and I gulped.

Then, almost as suddenly as it began, your hand released me, your eyes closed, and you settled into your body once more.

I took a deep breath, grinned, and began.

As I remembered to keep the 'angle of my dangle' at the requisite thirty degrees, I brought the cutting edge very slowly downward from cheekbone to jaw; pleased to see I left no mar, nor any cream.

The thick lather, emulsified as I mixed it, was the perfect consistency. It came off the razor into the bowl of water with a satisfactory plop. I rinsed the blade and returned for the next stroke.

Right cheek and jaw first; then left. Reaching across I again pressed myself to your arm, letting myself brush you gently with each movement of my hand across your face. The muscles of your jaw tensed; I paused; my blade held still until you settled again.

Just before I started under your neck, I repositioned myself. I threw one leg over both of yours to position your thighs between mine; then I sat down and moved forward so that I was nestled comfortably on your lap.

You reached down between my open thighs, causing me to catch and hold my breath.

Without opening your eyes, you grasped the newspaper beneath me and pulled. I chuckled when it does not come easily, but you persisted, so I leaned forward, pressing one hand to your chest as I held the blade a distance and lifted my behind.

Your hand was now trapped in the small opening of dark warmth between us. You groaned loudly, much to my delight.

You changed tactics, deciding to open your legs just slightly and let the paper fall to the floor. Laughing, I sat back and you returned your hand to its armrest. Then you seemed to reconsider and moved your hands to my hips, pulling me solidly forward. This time it is was I who groaned.

Eyes still closed you smirked but left your hands where they were. I cleared my throat and tried to focus.

I placed my left thumb under your chin and pushed it upward. Then I took the razor in my right hand again and began my first careful stroke.

Halfway up I stopped.

Holding it there, my heartbeat quickened and I felt myself bear ever so softly against the pulsing vein in your neck.

You gasped softly and your eyes flashed open. Holding my pressure steady, I grinned up at you devilishly through darkened lashes. One eyebrow rose as I willed you to challenge me.

Your hands dug into the flesh of my hips, but I did not relent.

I silently reminded you which of us is held at the mercy of the other, and I could see the struggle within you crest your face just after you realized I intended to grant no mercy.

Finally, you looked upward to the ceiling and sighed in resignation before your eyes closed and your hands released their grip.

I was freed to finish my work.

Once done, I slid off your lap and examined my handiwork, smoothing the warm wetness of a fresh towel across the lines of your beautiful face to clean away the last traces of any cream.

I moved behind and pressed the lever that raised the back of your seat. I reached over to pick up the hand mirror and placed it in your palm. You opened your eyes and brought it up for a look. You turn to check each side, paying particular attention to the underside of your neck. When you saw no mark, you smiled, caught my eye, and nodded in amusement.

I took the mirror from you and set it aside. Then just as you moved to sit forward, I put one palm to your chest and pushed you gently back.

You looked at me quizzically but did as I bid. I smiled as I move in front of you and lowered your seat to its lowest position. Then I place my hands on each of your knees, and slowly moved to part them.

I leaned down towards your feet, giving you a quick glimpse inside my blouse, as I folded the footrest up into its closed position.

I could feel the questions crowd your mind but was pleased that you decided to indulge me and see this through. I reached under the cloth that covered my side table and pulled out a velvet covered pillow.

I dropped it to the floor between your legs and knelt on it with my hands pressing on your thighs as I did.

Grinning, I reached up and unbuttoned the top few buttons of my blouse as I silently watched you watching me. Then, still watching you, I unclipped the front closure of my lace brassiere, but did nothing to completely shake myself free of it or open my blouse further.

Your grip tightened around the arms of your chair and you were visibly affected.

Slowly I reached for the waistband of your dark slacks. You barely noticed as your eyes seemed transfixed elsewhere, just as I had intended. Using both hands and causing my breasts to press naturally together between my upper arms, I unbuttoned the waist of your slacks before opening the zipper of your fly.

When I reached in to pull you free your focus broke and you moaned reflexively, nearly coming out of your seat as you did. Holding you with one hand, I reached into your pocket with the other and extracted the condom I knew you carried. I put it to my lips, tore it open, and place the delicate circle between my lips where I held it with care as I tossed the wrapper aside.

Then I lowered my mouth onto your waiting hardness and rolled it down as my mouth encompassed you, never using my hands.

When it was completely unfurled, I lifted my head and noticed sweat had begun to bead on your brow. I know too well the restraint you had to exercise.

'Hold me', I said, finally freeing you to do what I knew you held back. You moaned loudly as your hands dived in for my exposed flesh, burying themselves between the lace of each cup and the warm of my soft skin; the hardened nubs of your patient reward now pinched between thumbs and forefingers; their weight held in your cupped hands.

I returned to my own point of interest, and let you watch as I extracted the payment for my devoted attention. I was relentless as I demanded my price, and, finally, you cried out in release and unequivocally lost the control I was after.

You became putty in my hands once more.

And you were reminded, again, why you would have it no other way.

Melted Stone

I once came home late after a long day of meetings at the office and found my favorite fellow in his overlong smoking jacket, curled in a chair by the window.

The room was filled with candlelight and soft music was playing off in another room somewhere, gently wafting its tender tones down the hallway and creating a wonderful softness that enveloped me the moment I walked in the door.

This was exactly what I needed. This special place of my reprieve from the harshness of the world outside was precisely what would take me from the powered-up executive I enjoyed being, to the warm, soft, tender woman beneath.

I dropped my bag and kicked off my heels at the door, unbuttoned my jacket and headed over to my handsomely lazy lover. I sat on the floor at his feet, rested my head in his lap, sighed deeply, and let his touch begin to smooth the way for a wonderful evening. After a moment, he quietly said he had a surprise for me, so I lifted my heavy head to see his face as I wondered what magical things he had stored.

He softly opened his robe and showed me the red lace corset beneath, tears in her eyes at this great risk being taken.

A year we had been together, laughing and loving and sharing our innermost selves, our dreams, and our hopes. How could I have not foreseen this? And how, in a moment so tender, with her being so vulnerable, could I do anything but respond with love? If I loved her, wasn't I required to do so unconditionally?

If it took her a full year to reveal this part of herself wouldn't it be incredibly cruel and shaming if I did not embrace her – the one person she trusted so much?

I was trapped and unseated and sad for the direction I knew this would turn us, yet deeply respected her courage and bravery.

I did the only thing I knew I could do. I made love to the woman before me as best I knew how.

But, somewhere, somehow, I lost a piece of myself in the doing.

Normal

We seek to be that which others are
Or want from us
Aching
To be our
Selves

He pushes
Her mouth
Down there
Where she
Knows
She does not belong

Another she
Attempts entry
To doors that are
Closed
Places
She is unwelcome

And both sides are
Judged and
Condemned
For something
They are not

Until that union
Perfect
Mysterious
Stone soul
Union

She, stone
No longer shamed
Degraded
Forced and coerced
To giving "shoulds"

He, stone
No longer shamed
Degraded
Forced and coerced
To receive "shoulds"

Freed
To love as
And who
They are

Freed
To touch as
And who
They need

Exit-only

Meets

All-access-pass

And both

Find joy

Both

Suddenly

Find

Home

Greedy and Selfish

I once turned to a close friend, someone who had been my lover a dozen years before and asked her whether she thought it would be selfish of me if I decided I was stone. She responded with a very emphatic, "Yes!"

We discussed it a little more, and I tried to understand where her response originated. Did she think femmes were demanding and self-centered as a whole, and therefore any additional (and seemingly) femme-centered pleasures just too much? Or maybe it was that she was more strongly identified as a sexual bottom than I had previously known? I did not want to rule out that I might be considering my own stone sexuality for solely self-serving reasons – I really did need to understand.

I finally concluded that it did not matter how opposed she might be to femmes who identified as stone, nor how self-serving my self-discovery might seem. In this case self-serving was not based on ego or a lowered interest in my partner's fulfillment; being stone actually *was* my natural wiring.

I had done many things through the years to pleasure my partners, things based on passion and love that had nothing to do with my own eroticism or desire.

I loved; therefore, I gave. But without realizing it I had given things that took me further from my strongest self.

By claiming my stone identity, I was declaring that whether there be feast or famine I could no longer do or be anything other than my most authentic (stone) self.

If that meant there would be no lovers who would not judge me as greedy and selfish, then so be it.

I am happy to report that this life affirming, quite self-serving decision opened the door to the most fulfilling sexual experiences I have ever had.

It has been nothing but feasts ever since.

Stone Garden

Three mornings
I stared at the fence line
Willing the blooms
That existed only in my mind

Rows of red
Behind white
A pond of lilies
Nearby

But there were no stones
No markers
Of strength
No framing
For all my envisioned beauty

Then I thought, what is glory
Without hardness
What is color
Without the balance of grounded weight

I moved outside
Placed the stones as sentries
Stepped back
Smiling

This was what I needed

These soldiers my permission

To plant

And to finally

Find my way to bloom

What This Femme Wants

Though it might be an easy assumption, spoiling me is not something I'd put near the top of the list of things I want – although it's great when I get it occasionally, whether through attention, time together, or small surprises. I prefer a number of other things more. Most of the items on this list may not sound like ways I want someone to treat me, but trust me, if they have these qualities, I will get the treatment I am seeking.

These are things that will make me feel safe, like I am involved with a mature adult, someone who respects me because they have self-respect first:

- **Strength of character.** A partner who is comfortable saying no; someone who has thought about what they value most and are no longer willing to compromise. Any butch that has poked around and discovered what really matters to him, has had it challenged by friends or therapists extensively, and has come out the other end stronger and clearer about what is right and wrong for him is a real delight to be around. He is not on the defensive because he does not see differences as a personal challenge and walks a wide circle around behaviors and choices that lead him off his path.

- **Emotional autonomy.** Someone who does not "need" me. This does not mean he's emotionally unavailable or that my presence in his life doesn't compliment his, but rather that he feels full within himself and isn't looking at me to help create that fullness of spirit or Spirit. I may fill him from my cup at times, but he already fills his own. I can say to him, 'So, how do you want to handle that?' rather than, 'Here, let me take care of that for you.'

    This subtle difference inspires and delights him and affirms his strength. We all have times we need someone or where it would be appropriate to step up and take care of something for another, but there is much more mutual empowerment when I can trust he is strong enough to steer the biggest part of his life and he gives the same room for me.

- **Honest, without ever being brutal.** Someone with a tight muscle around being honest with others and a critical eye for what might hurt; a butch who knows that downplaying or stepping over the truth hurts us both.

I had a partner one time that I loved deeply, and one day he sat me down and very lovingly and gently told me he was 'done,' that the relationship had come to a close for him. Though incredibly stunned, I admired his honesty and delivery, even in the moment. I was devastated and had not seen it coming (we had been in counseling for a long time with little success because our sexual expressions were so different), but I didn't pressure to know why right then.

What did 'why' matter if that was really his truth? I could always ask later when emotions were calmer. What could I do but let him go? I have never regretted a moment we were together and yet I can see his wisdom in hindsight and will be forever grateful.

Attributes that make me feel special or cared for:

- **Intuition.** This is a hard one if it does not come naturally. I believe everyone is intuitive to a degree, but we grow up with our intuition ignored or discounted and somewhere along the way stop using it. So, it becomes a skill, something to be rediscovered and then relied on regularly until it strengthens.

Intuition is about knowing when to pause when something does not feel or sound quite right. Intuition is that gentle inner knowing that conveys there is a piece of information that needs special attention to right now or that is about to be overlooked and will be useful later. Having a well-developed sense of intuition is an important piece of having high emotional intelligence (a high "EQ").

- **Touch.** Seduction is so much more than the pursuit of my soft and womanly curves; it is about the way a butch makes an indelible impression on my mind.

  The easiest way to do this is by touching me — non-sexually, which is incredibly sexual. Catching and holding my eye when I least expect it, reaching out to tuck my hair behind my ear when we're talking, placing his tuxedo or bow tie draped over the bathroom mirror for me the morning after a wonderful night out. 'Steering' me through a crowd, invisibly reaching out a hand to draw me closer when a group or person's conversation has started to leave me out, et cetera.

  Sometimes the best 'touching' occurs without eye contact to support it. The butch who practices the art of touching me like this has gone a long way toward opening my heart and getting me to soften for him. I do believe it is something to be studied and practiced and few take the time to be good at it.

- **Leans or presses on me to drink in my loyalty, support, honesty, and compassion.** This may not sound like something that makes me feel special, but it does. I like feeling strong and competent, and I like very much being held to a high standard where love is concerned. This may be the most difficult to explain because it is more about a very subtle and often unconscious interchange that is going on.

  He *expects* and *trusts* me to be there for him, to have his back, to open to him when the world has turned him away, to become lovingly invisible when his hurts are too great to share. There is an element of using me entwined in this expectation, this 'giving' of his energy to me for safekeeping.

It makes me feel safe and strong and needed and valuable on some really exquisite level.

You either understand what I am talking about or not, I really cannot describe it any better.

Things I want/need relationally from a partner:

- **Emotional availability.** This means he is done his work. Certainly not every last piece of it, but quite a bit. By 'work' I mean he has uncovered and processed to death (in some form or fashion) any childhood issues with abuse, his parents, his gender dysphoria growing up, the religion he was or wasn't raised in, his relationship to God/Goddess/The Universe, his fears of failure and success, his relationship patterns, addictions, etc. If he and I do not have a clear grasp on who we each are how do we expect to be available to one another?

  Someone who has not done their work will not know how to swim out of the muddy waters when we get overwhelmed or start to drown. He will not be able to see past his "stuff." (Not that we do not all get like that sometimes, but certainly not regularly.) I need help nourishing the relationship and maneuvering the difficulties that love rises and a bowl that has been scrubbed clean holds more clear water than one that is still caked in mud.

- **Room to give.** This one goes hand in hand with emotional availability. A partnership requires giving and receiving to keep it rich. If he is not comfortable receiving or receives more than he gives (whether he is aware of it or not) the relationship eventually topples from imbalance.

  I have a need to give, a need to be open. I need to know I matter, that my gifts matter.

  When a butch shuts out the harming world he sometimes shut me out with it. It gets even more complicated when there is the appearance that he's open, but there is a push-pull because he really isn't.

When my giving is invisible (which has been an ongoing problem with femmes) I can easily give too much and later resent it or feel used. Likewise, when I have the appearance of giving, but I do not equally receive, then I also push-pull because I am not truly open.

- **Teamwork.** Rarely do we use this word in relationship to coupling, but my friends that are most happily mated are great at teamwork. Working together in unison to accomplish a mutual goal is a lofty romantic premise that often requires sacrifice and effort by both parties to achieve.

One couple I knew were under contract to buy their first home when the femme's mother died. The time off cost the femme her job, but their partnership was still in its' early years so the butch really did not want to pay the entire down payment alone.

Since the femme had wanted to transition into self-employment full-time anyway, she tapped into her resources: other femmes. One wrote copy for her marketing materials almost overnight, others gathered up all their contacts to overwhelm her with new business, and in less than a few months the femme came up with the $10k she needed.

When they closed on the house, the butch, who did technical work from home, surprised the femme by paying to have the in-law unit converted into a studio for her new business as a gift and instead works out of a small corner of the den.

Their goal was to share as partners in purchasing a home and each was willing to do what they could to make it work for the other. In this case, the butch's fiscal boundaries gave him a chance to see what his partner's contribution to their marriage would be and he found a way to appreciate her for it.

Critical requirements for greatest success:

- **Equality.** This might sound like many of the others, but it is not. Partners can enjoy all sorts of dynamics, like daddy/girl, butch/femme, and dominant/ submissive, though without each person's contribution being equal over time, it is doomed from the start.

  Sometimes my needs take precedence over my partner's; at other times it is his. The point is that each of us appreciates and feeds the other and the energy exchanged is kept in balance.

  Equality is about more than equal contributions and the balance of power; it is also about starting (and working) from equal positions. I may enjoy some occasional consensual power exchanges, but if my partner does not have personal power equal to mine the scales will always be tipped.

  'Partnership' requires each person step up to the starting line with complementary capacities to give, receive, grow, and nourish each other. It is only within this balance of equity that both parties will eventually share fully the fruits of their investments.

- **Empathy, combined with vital force.** When I was quite young, I was partnered with a butch whose mother required him to wear a dress or "at least" face makeup to soften his masculine looks when they were together. I went along with at it first, not wanting to undermine his right to decide for himself what was okay for him and what was not.

  After one of these family visits, he came home angry, trying to cover over the tears he later cried. As he lay in my arms and I tried to soothe him as best I could, something in me snapped. I drew him up, arms on either shoulder, and looked him square in the eye. I said, "You will NEVER wear a dress or makeup again. Not for anybody! DO YOU HEAR ME?"

  My energy sliced right through any resistance or excuses he might have had. It was empathy that drove me, but it was in combination with vital force that it made the real difference.

He knew it was over; that my words had somehow released him and he never, *ever* wore anything feminine from that day forward. I have seen femmes do this kind of work repeatedly.

I want a partner who shares this skill. Someone who looks for the way they can protect me from whatever harms, even if that something is me.

- **Independent interests.** I saved this one for last, but it is the one that really helps keep things juicy. This is the breathing room that helps keep us from collapsing in on ourselves.

I want a butch who is so supportive of this concept that they actually require that we have some things and friends we generally keep apart. Not in a secretive I-need-to-be-separate-so-you-don't-need-to-know-or-can't-EVER-come-with-me way, but rather someone who enjoys that we each go off and do things that we get to come back and talk about later.

It is stimulus that keeps our connection interesting; something that provides the mystery that is so important to maintaining curiosity and heat.

Betty and Bob

I'm sitting at a table with just two chairs, a little crust of a café table top with three legs that wobble because one lost its felt pad the first year we got it; me and Betty, who is outside right now writing me her Sunday letter, same as she's done for the past near forty years. It's gotten to be that I wait for them, 'specially after the doc's last visit when he told us she should start "getting things in order."

Getting things in order my ass. Like her cupboards are in disarray or her flowers aren't planted straight. Harrumph I say. The only thing in need of getting in order around here is his frisky hands. He took too much time looking for her heartbeat, that's what needs getting' in order, I think.

Betty comes to me when I get flustered like this. Swings up close and places her hand on my chest, up a little high like she always does, almost seeming to know too low would make me move it away. She never once made *that* mistake, and never once said I had anything but a "chest." I love her for that; not just calming me down and helping me to see my way to forgive'n, but for knowing what soft looks and careful hands will do to swell my heart, 'specially when she folds herself in close. Makes me feel strong and right. Like I'm taller or smarter somehow. Betty always does that.

I reach in my pocket, pull out matches I swiped somewhere from a long dead smoker's habit, tore off a little piece of the white cover, leavin' just enough to still fold it shut (like that mattered) and slipped it under the edge of the too-short table leg. The damn thing's been around almost as long as I have and fallin' apart just as fast, and *now* I'm finally fix'n it. She'll give me heck for that.

Once in a while, I hear her pen scratchin' and let myself wonder what she's makin' it say. Betty's not one for lily ponds or moonlight, but damn fire if she still don't manage to make it sound like she's whipped me with honey once she's done. I'll laugh and grin, slap my knee (which always starts her off smilin') and then won't be able to talk for a while for the stranglehold her words put round my heart.

When I'm done I'll fold the letter up careful, shake my head like I'm dashin' flies off it, clear my throat to ease the tightness in it, stand up slow without meeting her eye (though I know she's watching me out the corner of it). Then I'll walk into the back room to put it with the others in tall, neat rows of shoeboxes that are stacked near waist high in rows of two at the bottom of my closet.

She doesn't know, but sometimes when the moon is so loud I can't sleep, I sneak to the back room, light one of them old lamps with green glass turned black from soot and reread the latest and greatest in my swelling collection.

I'm about as proud of those letters as any man has ever been of his child, '57 Chevy, or yes, even his Harley. There's a bit of me writ into every one; she gave them birth, nurtured 'em into life, but tucked here or there she makes references to field flowers I picked or the ripe plum I dripped in her mouth near the falls one hot summer as I squished it's juice through my fingers, just to see how it's red water looked on her open lips.

Betty writes moments we share, turns them into golden sunshine and silver liquid. It still makes me try to dream up more, to bring her moments that matter enough to have her want to put them to the page.

It's my job to make sure she's safe and protected, sheltered from big cities, fast talkers, and harm. The easiest way to do that, other standing guard all the time (especially with doctors who get too friendly), is to bring her sweetness.

Sweet plums, sweet smelling flowers, sweet jars of jam. If I can buy, barter, or make it, it's hers. I get bona fide pleasure from seeing her melt, watching the way her eyes and face sparkle, the way she sort of just "opens up" and takes the thing or experience in, the way she tries to tuck her face when it gets to her so much she cries. Well, and maybe I *do* get a *little* pleasure from hearing her tell tales about it in a letter on Sundays that follow.

You see, sweetness builds her buffer to the world. When days and weeks are filled with sweet experiences and tender offerings, especially from someone close like me, well, life and death stuff don't get the same grip.

Sure, sure, life is hard sometimes and losing someone or something you love's even harder, but when you've been filled up like that you fall back on satin pillows, rather than catchin' a broken tailbone 'cause life dealt one more cruel blow. When people get shored up over and over and over, it don't take 'em long to remember the world's a good place when bad news comes their way. So, the way I see, that's about as important and any other kind of protection Betty deserves.

"Bob, can I get some tea?" Johnny asks as he passes me on his way to the kitchen, snapping me out of my reverie and it dawnin' on me I was so lost in my thoughts I didn't even hear the screen door slam.

"Sure, help yourself. But don't touch the cookies. Hear?"

I heard his grumbling but couldn't make out any dissent. A minute or so later he returned, a tall glass of lemon tea in one hand, a teaspoon in the other. He sat down and I saw his cheeks looked full, his mouth dusted suspiciously with crumbs. I scowled at him and brought my fist down on the table hard. The sugar bowl kicked its lid almost clean off as Johnny's eyes got big.

"What'd I tell you?"

He struggled to swallow the dry cookie whole before he realized the tea would help wash it down.

"I *told* you!"

"But...but...I just had one," he choked out before a fit of coughing overtook him. Tea sprayed out his nose.

Served him right, I thought.

"Betty! Betty!" I hollered out. "I told the boy to leave 'em alone and did he listen?" I glared back at him as he cower'd rightly enough.

Betty opened the screen door and walked in, her paper and pen in her left hand, her right holding the screen door behind her to make sure it closed without its bang.

"Now would you look there!" I motioned at Betty to all who would see, boring my eyes into Johnny's with a feigned look of disgust. "You messed up everything! Ruined my Sunday letter! Hell's bells—she'll never get it finished now and that'll ruin a perfect run! Never missed a one Betty hasn't and here you come cookie theifin' like some hillbilly barn boy stealing cherry pie from a windowsill and ruinin' everything!"

By now his coughing fits had subsided and his tea was half drunk without its pound of sugar he always added.

"Let the boy alone Bob. He don't mean no harm." Betty said as she leaned over and rustled her hand through the top of Johnny's hair as she kissed his forehead at the crown.

Johnny smiled. Then had the nerve to grin. I scowled deeper.

"You're lucky she favors you... scallywag!" I was trying hard to keep the gruff up, but it was fading fast in favor of a grin seeing the youngun I'd come to think of as my son.

"I'm sorry Pops."

There, that did it. I loved being called Pops more than just about anything. I stood up and turned to catch Betty as she walked by, tryin' to hide my grin.

Pulling her hips back toward me I growled in her ear, "And just where you going missy?" I loved her jasmine smell.

She half-heartedly swatted at me and wriggled out of my reach.

"Now you know good and well Sunday letters are mine 'till I finish 'em—which may be never at the rate you're going!" she teased me as she headed for the back hallway and out the back door.

"Yeah, well I wish you'd finish with *your* Sunday letters so I can have *mine*," I hollered toward the now closed door.

I sighed and turned around, plopping heavily in my chair again.

This time the table didn't wobble.

Butch Appreciation Day

A group of girls and I were once discussing how difficult it must be for our guys to walk through the world, their differences flagged for the entire world to see and mock and ridicule at every turn.

Public bathrooms a daily struggle – whether to go and face myriad confrontations or avoid going and risk poor health. Bio families that were endlessly estranged for lack of understanding and compassion. Bodies that betrayed the sense of self that lay beneath. Hecklers on city streets; men jealous of the women who loved them and claimed space on their arms.

It took little effort to convince ourselves to don our best dresses and give them a party. We wanted a way to show them we valued their bravery and courage. They needed to know we got them.

The day was fraught with preparation. Heels, feather boas, and lipstick for some, Chapstick and jeans for others. We baked pies and cookies, mixed beverages, created an altar in homage to all things butch, strung decorations, and prepared to give the show of our lives.

When our handsome guests arrived, we were ready.

In they came by singles, pairs, and groups. On motorcycles in leather, in top hats and ascots, in Levis and flannel shirts – we had them all. It was the grandest parade of masculinity I had ever seen. Their manner was courteous, appreciative, and curious. Ours was reverent and devoted.

They were our heroes and we desperately wanted them to know it.

Once our guests had all arrived, a few gals were scattered among the boys to hand feed them chocolate-dipped fruit or tiny pastries, while others prepared themselves backstage.

The show folded in on itself with grace, humor, sultriness, and sass. We came bearing an erotic dance, readings and poetry of exaltation, skits of hilarity, and songs conveying admiration and praise, each one garnering more applause than the one before.

When it was over the guys asked if they might have a few minutes to share with us the impact this had for them, so we moved to join them and obliged.

They told us (some with big beefy tears) how desperately they needed this and never knew it.

They told us how lonely their struggles had been and how little understood they felt even by those that shared their lives. One fellow said he would never again be the same; that this moment had given him a permission he didn't realize was missing.

By the time they were through we began to comprehend how magical this day had become.

I think we were all changed by it.

As the afternoon faded into evening and the fellows partook in the remaining festivities we had planned, I sat back and said a little prayer of thanks.

I never knew how profoundly grateful one could feel for having an opportunity to appreciate another.

Lusty Slivers

In my luxuriously lazy and
Complicated way
I examine the almond I adore

Rough and ready brown
Protects the cream
As it slowly slides between pink, wet lips

A familiar want is stirred
Of other shells
And other hardened cores

Letting my mind walk
As my body is rent
And I am carried from nothing

To desire

Olives and Pearls

I watched you come in. You did not see me, but I saw you. It was your hair I noticed first, more silver than it had been some ten years before.

My Latin Love. That is what I called you then. I wondered if this new woman had a lover's name for you.

I watched you for a while, my heart tugging uncomfortably with each tender touch of her arm. When you guided her out to dance and one finger took the slow path from her shoulder blade to hip, I shivered, remembering how it felt.

I lifted my near empty glass, let the two pearl onions roll into my mouth, and motioned to Rosie for another.

Damn, that had been harder to see than I thought.

Sometimes a butch had a word or a phrase that made your knees give, sometimes it was a look. Few knew the power of a signature touch.

You had mastered them.

There were at least three or four that I could remember. The 'back trail' that told me you thought me sexy, proud to be showing me off; the encircled wrist to tell me I was owned; the folded kisses in my palm before work or trips away to "save for later". And my all-time favorite: when you placed my hand flat to the center of your bound chest, letting me feel your heartbeat and willing me to know it was also owned.

That one was hardest earned. I lay in your arms and opened to you every night for two years before you gave it to me.

My new drink came, and I gulped it greedily. Rosie knew two olives always followed two pearls on Thursday nights. It was my secret butch/femme joke.

Never before had I been so glad that I had taken space in this last booth, favored for its darkness and view. Sitting here I was overlooked by most, still seeing all the action.

Lovers' quarrels, catty queens, the shot slams, and the subtle or not-so-subtle cruising. I came out of my cave only once or twice a night, when the liquor got to be too much and the jane was empty, which didn't always happen in unison.

Weekends were different. I'd gussy up and put on my glam like any other gal, flirted and bantered with the best of 'em. But Thursdays were painful and dark. 'Girls night out' I called them, though I was the only girl.

In a million years, I could not imagine you would show up here. You'd stopped coming when I moved out; bitter and angry, humiliated by my sudden departure.

As I watched your girl salsa and move with you in ways my white rhythm-less body had failed, I was dragged helpless by demons through a crusty old wound.

We had been happy, deliriously so. Parties for a hundred; barbeques for ten; movies and dinners out with our closest pals. I loved you in black, you loved me in red.

I was new, excited by your firm touch and hard ways; near fainted at your machismo. Jealous? No, not much, but I sure knew how to stoke that fire in you. And there was little you weren't jealous of when it came to my attention.

Mi chica crema. My little cream. That's what you called me. I was cream for you alright. Baby cream, drunk on the discovery of my femmeness.

The Women's Resource Center opened and everything changed. Or, to be fair, it was the class I took that did it.

Smart, powerful women in Dietrich pin-striped suits, French twists, and neutral lipstick told me about butch/femme history, our *herstory*. They were academics, big-brained and book-learned. Sharp as nails without any. They pushed me to think, to see the world, my world, in ways I'd failed to see.

My face burned hot the night they told me that those like you were the disfigured arms of men, that your control of me was wrong. I remember thinking what a fool I'd been.

I now hated the very things I once loved.

I was quiet that night, too quiet. You thought I'd met someone, forbid me to go again, certain you'd been betrayed; that someone had touched what was *yours*. Those words bit and cut me deep. They proved the truth, that the Dietrichs had been right. I owned me! No one else! I was a womyn, not just a wo-*man* and I was bitter at the lies and illusion of your love. I had never questioned your stone, had never seen it as control of me, as denial of my love for other womyn.

Now I did.

The poison of my newfound knowledge ripped us apart. I am still ashamed of my challenges and taunts, my demented demands to let me touch you to prove your love.

You slapped me. I cried.

I called my new friends.

You turned your back, then went for a drive.

They moved my righteousness out within the hour. I was gone for good before you got back.

It was a conversation overheard in a community hot tub three lovers later before I suddenly saw who was saint and who the sinner.

But it was too late.

Too much was undone; too many hands had entered the places where once only you had tread.

I drank my tears. And still drink them on nights like this.

Sure, I had found my way back to my own stone, but I could never shake that what–if ghost. Even just last year I'd placed things you'd given me along my mantle. A silent tribute to My First.

I looked up from my cloudy haze just as you drew her hand to your chest. You danced like that for a moment, eyes locked, feet and world forgotten. My sadness deepened before it turned and shifted.

I cried slow, thin tears. Down one cheek and then the other. Happy to see you had healed enough to love again, sad that it wasn't me.

The song ended and your hand circled her wrist as you led her urgently out the door. Flushed and smiling, eyes glowing, she stretched after her purse as you passed it.

I downed my drink then nodded for another.

Two more olives, two more pearls.

Sanctuary

You promised
There'd be a room
Saved
A place
Where my discarded stockings
Would forever
Circle slowly on the ceiling fan
A place where I'd be safe
Saved only for me

When I'm tired
I remember your strength
I melt into
The embrace
Of your memory
Your arms
My powerful harbor
My haven

No matter how far
I travel
No matter the greatness
Of the seas I cross
I know
You stand
Silently

Waiting
Longing
My
Return

And it is my strength
To know you do

Lucy Goes Camping

One of the rites-of-passage many femmes travel is the road to feeling competent. So often we're socialized into deferring heavy or masculine tasks to others thought more capable.

We are not usually encouraged to become comfortable with table saws, our own car repairs, lifting bundles of wood, or hanging our own drapes. In my early years of becoming comfortably competent I often erred on the side of comedy.

Camping was no exception.

Having spent almost every childhood summer at various campgrounds, I grew up loving the outdoors. For several years, my partner and I at the time went tent camping with a large group of our friends at least a dozen or so weekends a year during the milder weather.

One day I decided I had had enough; no more would a tent force me to wiggle my jeans on lying down, and with no place to hang a mirror. I was no sissy – I didn't need a hair dryer or room service – but I'll be damned if that meant I needed to be unnecessarily awkward.

So, before our next trip I informed my handsome fellow that I was headed to the store to buy a femme-friendly tent, and he smirked, offering to come along to watch. I swatted at him and walked out the door, shoulders squared and quite determined.

Once at the camping goods store, I went up and down each isle of tents looking for one tall enough to stand in comfortably, and easy enough to put up alone if need be.

After deciding on two pop up versions, I called the clerk over and asked him to put them together so I could make my final selection. He rubbernecked a look at me, but I held firm. I think he did it more in response to my brazenness than anything.

After he had them both set up, I stepped inside each. I

chose the one that had a small loop just inside at eye level – a place to hang the mirror was a nonnegotiable, remember?

On our next camp outing I had a fresh mani/pedi, my hair was in curls tumbled about my shoulders, and I was wearing a long light blue denim gypsy skirt with a crisp white men's button-up tied under my breasts, the sleeves rolled to my elbows, flat brown sandals on my feet. I was ready and armed for business.

I pulled my tent from the bed of the truck and several of our gang jumped to assist, but I would not hear of it. They looked at each other, grinned, and shrugged. Within moments they had pulled up chairs to get the front row view.

Now that I had an audience, I was determined I would die before I would give up or be rescued. I *would* do this. And look good doing it, all else be damned.

First, I gathered and tossed away the stones and bramble in the spot I had selected – and I noticed happily my red nails were in wonderful contrast. After a few minutes, I gathered my hair up, twisted it into a bun, and stuck a pencil in it. It was getting in the way.

I tossed out the too-big tarp I'd purchased, went from one side to another until I had it smoothed out and tucked into the size I needed; all of which was met with welcomed catcalls when forward bending gave them a better view of my cleavage, or cheers when I did something particularly adept.

I tried hard to recall everything I had seen them do over the years. I was particularly grateful that they overlooked any ineptness and seemed to want to see me succeed.

Next the tent.

Three poles for a two-pole dome was a little confusing, but I was adamantly opposed to reading the directions and tried to recall how I had seen it done.

I assembled each of the long ones, seeing the ends (so far

away) disappearing into the bush. With the tent laid flat and the door facing the campfire some distance away, I knew I had the basics right.

I stopped for a few minutes to catch my breath but decided to disguise my need for oxygen and time to think by reaching behind my head to gather up the falling tendrils and try to work them back into my updo.

Now on to the more difficult part. Inserting those dab-blamed tent poles and popping the thing up.

I tried to be smart about it.

First one front corner, then the other pole at the opposing front corner, crisscrossing at the tent's midpoint as they lay atop it.

Now to the back corners.

I took one and tried to bend it and bend it and bend it, but each time I got it near the necessary hole it would snap downward on its side and the opposite end would come loose – much to the delight of all who watch.

Back and forth I went a couple of times, until some of my younger pals began to offer to help. They were quickly squelched by my partner who knew this was important to me. He had faith. And that faith gave me the courage I needed to finish.

I would do this. I would.

I stepped back for a minute, surveyed the scene, dusted off my skirt, and toweled the back of my neck, like I had just come out of round three with Rocky Balboa.

I knew what I needed!

I went over to one end, buried the pole end in the dirt, walked to the other end of the pole, and slipped it in the grommet, walked back to where I started, pulled that end from of the dirt and slipped it home as well. The crowd was on their feet roaring cheers and shouting words of encouragement. My hair was now in complete disarray, but I didn't care.

I repeated my steps with the second pole, both poles still lying on their sides arching flat and horizontal. I stepped back, scratching my head briefly while I tried to figure out what to do next when my pals came up to cheer me, pat my back, and tell me how close I was to winning. Their enthusiasm was all I needed to jump in the ring one last time. With a flourishing leap and a dazzling smile, I move forward, reached down, pulled one pole upward and – *wa-la!* The dome was up!

Knockout!

I am not sure who was prouder, me or my guy. His eyes burned with a new appreciation, and though I might never want to repeat my experience – I now knew I could if I needed.

I passed him the third pole, plopped in an open chair, sighed wearily, and said:

"Finish her up, babe."

Mercy

I exited the morning bath tying the robe at my waist, still rather pink and pruney and flushed.

This robe was my favorite. Nearly translucent pink cotton, so light and finely woven that it was softer than any high-end sheets I'd ever slept in. A gift from my favorite guy, who said he picked it because it matched my nails. With just an hour before I was due at the office, I sat down at the vanity and began the application of my "natural" beauty.

A few small dips into a small silver jar of moisturizer, then the delicate eye cream for base, followed by a gentle layer of foundation with a sable brush.

Behind me, he stirred in the sheets, turning to watch as I knew he would. This was one of our most private dances, and one that occasionally cost us dearly when it carried us away. I always sought to watch him put on his butch; the jeans or slacks, the boots, the button up shirt or tee, his leather belt – and he never failed to audience me with the reciprocal awe and heat when I put on my femme.

I smiled to myself and sighed happily inside as I leaned forward and looked in the mirror. I drew out a slender brush from the cup, dabbed it in brown eye shadow and applied it softly. One eye, then the other.

A second slim brush brought a subtle highlight, a third dusted rose blush on my cheeks, under my chin for softening, and just to the sides of my forehead to mask its width. I added pencil liner along my outer eyes, brushed my brows with a soft brown, and added light strokes of dark mascara before finishing with a pink-tinted neutral lipstick for the day.

That final touch brought a low, restless groan from the bed. But I refused to be undone. I had a conference call planned in forty minutes during the drive in.

I pulled each clip from my hair, a little slower than I might have normally, savoring the feeling of being watched be someone I so adored. There is little I wouldn't do to affect him given the opportunity.

I reached for my hairbrush and began to bring it down through my tresses. He moved out of bed wearing only a white tee and matching boxer briefs, came to stand behind me quietly, and said, "Here, let me."

I caught his eyes in the mirror and held them as I passed the brush back over my shoulder.

He smiled, moved his gaze to the task at hand, and then carefully, with one hand under the weight of each section, brought the strokes from top to end with steadied and protracted smoothness.

I closed my eyes and let myself luxuriate in the experience; let his wonder bleed into and through me, filling me up and igniting a fire that would simmer and flare at its will. I let my arms fall to my sides and reached my hands back and wrapped them around each of his strong calves, letting my nails dig in softly whenever the goose bumps on my neck were raised by his touch.

Nirvana for us both.

Finally, the time pressed in on me and I knew if I did not stop us now I soon couldn't.

I let go of his legs and leaned gently away from him, playfully shooing him as I did.

He laid the brush on my table, pulled my hair back once more, and then brought his lips to my warm neck. I moaned reflexively, which only served to encourage him. His arms slipped downward and found their way inside my robe.

Then, unsatisfied, he pulled it open wide and exposed me to the mirror before us. I gasped and melted against his hands, helpless to stop the power now raging between us. I was bared to his gaze and my cheeks reddened as nether parts swelled heavy and full. I had to look away as his eyes and hands devoured me, his mouth still engulfing my neck.

But then I remembered again my morning agenda. I begged him to stop, but he grinned first with his eyes before whispering, "Say it."

I groaned, hating that he called me out. Rarely was it I that was cornered first. Oh, how many times it had been *he* who called the magic word that ended our games – almost never me – so he relished those moments all the more. He used them to strut and tease for days.

And now here I was, trapped by our shared desired, between the intoxication of his love and the sobriety of my work.

"Okay, okay... *Mercy*."

He released me immediately and belly laughed his way back to the edge of the bed. I was furious. Maybe this had been his only intent all along. I quietly picked up my hairbrush and threw it, just missing his ducked head. His laughter grew stronger.

Alright, so he wanted to play, did he? I'd remind him who was queen of the games. How easily he forgets.

I pulled my robe closed, then thought better of it. I turned around to face him and opened it again, then reached to cinch the belt tightly under my heavy breasts now fully exposed. He sucked in his breath and went quiet.

Without dropping eye contact I reached back, opened one of the drawers, and pulled out two silk stockings. His breathing deepened causing me to smile sweetly.

His eyes followed my hands as I rolled one down and prepared to let my toes enter it. Then I carefully raised it over foot, ankle, lower then upper calf, over the knee, and slowly, slowly up and around my thigh. My pointed toes rested on the bed's corner between his legs as I silently dared him not to touch me.

Then the second leg was done just the same, pausing here or there to stroke out imaginary wrinkles.

He reached for my legs, the ache to touch them now too

much.

"Uh-uh," I tsked reprovingly.

His hands backed away. He knew everything would stop if he did not heed my warnings.

When both stockings were in place I stood, reached into the drawer again, and withdrew the cream garter. Knowing he was always allowed to assist, he grinned. I handed him the belt, stepped forward between his open legs, and brought my private scent close enough to press his face against it, causing him to groan.

He would pay in every way possible for making me say that word. I'd make certain of it.

I pulled the length of the robe up and out of the way, baring myself to him once more. He choked on a cough and then brought the belt around my hips to clasp its closure. I let my free hand roam his hair as he did, tempting myself to push his head towards my moistened sex.

Once hooked, he turned it round me to ensure the closure was in back, and then moved to clasp each of the front metal clips over the silk.

When that task was complete, and he was clearly salivating from the confusion of warring against his desire, I turned around so he had access to the rear clips. But rather than make it easier for him to find his composure, I decided to raise the stakes one more time.

I moved to spread my feet a few extra inches apart, bent over fully, and arched my back. He groaned deeply knowing this time it would be impossible to resist.

I wiggled my hips very, very slowly; daring my scent to find his flared nostrils, knowing he'd play havoc trying to get the back clips to meet their mark, now so much further away than where they usually connected.

I looked over one shoulder, caught his eye, and said, "Help me."

He groaned yet again, brought his hands up to rub against his face as if to wash it free from thoughts clouding in as he tried desperately to regain some balance. He still had a task to do.

Though not easy by a long shot, he finished his assignment to my satisfaction, now thinking he was free.

But he was wrong. There was still so much more I wanted to have. He hadn't paid nearly enough.

I turned around, un-cinched my robe and let it fall to the floor. Then I moved to sit, straddling his thighs, my warmth now opened fully between us. I leaned forward, allowed myself to drink from his lips, and let his hands encircle my waist as he tried to bring me close.

But I stopped him. I wanted just enough distance.

Still claiming his mouth as mine, I reached one of my hands down between us and began to stroke within my wetness.

His hands flexed tighter when he realized what I was doing and he growled deeper into our kiss, now taking it from me.

I continued as I softened and let him consume my mouth. I stroked, over and over, deeper, and deeper, the wetness now audible to us both.

His left hand roamed and claimed my chest as his right hand fought to pull me ever closer to the hardness I knew was now growing within him. I melted against him as his energy swirled to surround and shelter me, letting my hand move furiously to its needy end while I surrendered with my mouth, my little moans...my sweet breath.

When I peaked, his need for me had flamed so violently that he ravaged my mouth, my neck, my breasts – there was no place he would not claim and consume and I was powerless to stop him.

Then I shivered and quaked my sudden frailness more fully against him, and his movements and touches turned sweet. He protected me. He always protected me in those final moments.

But I was not done.

Instantly my power returned and my hand moved and shifted from my wet to his hard. The length of his hardness was a wonderful contrast for my wet hand. I ran the length of it still beneath his briefs and saw him begin to swim. I pushed its base against him several times to let him find that rhythmic grove that I know brings his release, but then stopped just short.

I wanted to see.

I stood and moved back just enough to open his legs and kneel between them. I pulled him free, and then delivered a frustrating glance up at him when I realized he wasn't sheathed. He said hang on one sec as he leaned over the bedside and quickly reappeared with the needed condom.

I grinned.

I ripped open the package, placed the reservoir end in my mouth, and then rolled it down his length with my lips. We both loved when I did that.

For several long minutes, I let my mouth explore and reacquaint itself with his member. I loved that he allowed me this access, loved more how much he needed it, but my favorite was how quickly it powered him up.

After four rapid strokes his hands moved into position and he took over. One on the back of my head caught deeply in my hair for control, the other at my chin to pry me open for greater depth. In these moments I went from taking pleasure to being used. And I loved it.

He would push, I would take all that I could, he would want more, I would choke a brief moment before I adjusted, then he would push and open me deeper. There was only his need.

Nothing else existed.

One or two minutes of this was all he needed to find the

first of thirty releases if that is what he desired. My knees would go numb before he'd quit given the opportunity. And he was close, so very, very close to that first one. I felt it rising, his body tensing, and my pleasure deepening and open, ready to receive the energy he needed to pump into my mouth.

But not today, my love.

I slowed, pulled back gently, and stood up.

Leaning down to kiss him adoringly despite his massive disorientation, I petted his check softly, and said, "Gotta' run."

Conclusion

If you have enjoyed this collection of writings, please be sure to leave an Amazon review, however brief, while the content is still fresh in your mind.

ABOUT THE AUTHOR
Victoria Anne Darling

Victoria Anna Darling has been a writer, educator, organizer, and beautifier for more than 25 years. She founded San Francisco's Femme Posse, the Butch/Femme Salons, the Butch/Femme Barter List, and the first-ever Butch Appreciation Day in 2002, which is now an international day.

Victoria is single, and, after leaving executive roles, has spent the last five years traveling across 48 of the United States. She also traveled to Hawaii, Europe, Mexico, and Cuba several times. She now resides in a 200-year-old farmhouse on 100 acres where she sips tea as she watches the sun and moon rise and set every day, hikes through the cornfields, and finds inspiration for her writings.

୧꧁ꕥ꧂୨

If you would like to be added to the author's email list to learn of new books as they are published, please send your name and any comments or feedback to: StoneProudAuthor@gmail.com.

Additional books currently available by this author:

Pillow Princesses & Touch-Me-Nots: Fuck You! Fuck You! Stonefemmes and Stonebutches are Taking These Terms Back!

The Stone Shelter: A Stonebutch/Stonefemme Love Affair

I Believe in Me! (A fully illustrated children's book on self-selecting pronouns, gender identity, gender expression, and sexuality in relaxed and easy ways, as part of daily living.)

You can also find them on the author's website at:

www.VictoriaAnneDarling.com